T0280051

HIDDEN
HISTORY
of
GRAND RAPIDS

HIDDEN
HISTORY
of
GRAND RAPIDS

Matthew A. Ellis

THE
History
PRESS

Published by The History Press
Charleston, SC
www.historypress.com

Copyright © 2023 by Matthew A. Ellis
All rights reserved

Front cover: Water Department laying water main. *Grand Rapids City Archives and Records Center.*

First published 2023

Manufactured in the United States

ISBN 9781467153041

Library of Congress Control Number: 2022944972

Notice: The information in this book is true and complete to the best of our knowledge. It is offered without guarantee on the part of the author or The History Press. The author and The History Press disclaim all liability in connection with the use of this book.

All rights reserved. No part of this book may be reproduced or transmitted in any form whatsoever without prior written permission from the publisher except in the case of brief quotations embodied in critical articles and reviews.

For my dear wife, Ashley,
without whose support, I would have faltered
and our four huskies,
Eros, Green Bean, Indigo and Xander.
I can't play fetch right now, but maybe later.

CONTENTS

Aerial view of downtown Grand Rapids, 2013. *Grand Rapids City Archives and Records Center.*

INTRODUCTION

Grand Rapids is a city of just under two hundred thousand. Nestled in the Grand River Valley and centered in West Michigan, the city is roughly thirty miles from the shore of Lake Michigan. The city is known today as Beer City for its myriad craft breweries and as an international art hub for its ArtPrize competition, the largest in the world. Many well-known individuals are associated with Grand Rapids, from the thirty-eighth president of the United States, Gerald R. Ford, to the Red Hot Chili Peppers' lead singer, Anthony Kiedis. The great American poet Henry Wadsworth Longfellow, however, is not regularly associated with Grand Rapids.

Yet, a sculpture of Longfellow has stood in Veterans Memorial Park, near the heart of Grand Rapids, for over one hundred years. The poet's bronze bust sits atop a marble pedestal, mirrored by a second, that of Thomas D. Gilbert. While Gilbert was a well-known citizen of the city, having settled there in 1855, and was almost solely responsible for the longevity of the park, Longfellow may have never visited the city. However, it seems Grand Rapidians had an affinity for the poet.

An article in the *Grand Rapids Herald* from 1900 recounted the story of a group of local schoolchildren spontaneously and simultaneously reciting Longfellow's poem "The Village Blacksmith." When Loraine Pratt Immen, who donated Longfellow's bust, dedicated the sculpture in 1912, she stated, "Citizens of Grand Rapids, I present this bust of Longfellow to you. Guard and treasure it and as often as you bid it 'good morning' or 'good night' do not forget his great words."[1]

Loraine Pratt Immen was an expert on Longfellow. She was an expert in general on great poets, orators and bards. In 1887, Immen organized a Shakespeare class for the Ladies Literary Club. This class eventually turned into a club in its own right. Immen presided as president of the Ladies Literary Club from 1889 to 1890 and was elected a vice president of the Woman's Rights Club when members organized the group in 1874. City directories listed Immen's profession as elocutionist. In 1895, she became a director of the National Association of Elocutionists. The newspapers recall countless events where she recited Shakespeare, Dickinson and Longfellow. She even gave lectures on Presidents Abraham Lincoln and George Washington.

Bronze statue of Henry Wadsworth Longfellow presented by Loraine Pratt Immen. *Grand Rapids City Archives and Records Center.*

Immen's husband, Frederick, was born in Germany in the 1830s and immigrated to the United States as a young boy. He became a carpet dealer and later a general importer, amassing a small fortune. He owned multiple buildings in downtown Grand Rapids, including 126 Monroe Avenue NW, renting some out to other shopkeepers. Frederick and Loraine had two children, Arthur and Elmer. Elmer died in infancy. Arthur suffered from ailments throughout his childhood and eventually succumbed to his maladies in 1893, when he was twenty. Frederick passed away in 1909.

Loraine lavished her wealth on Grand Rapids and sought to honor her lost family. She donated heavily to the Ladies Literary Club and other charities. For Christmas in 1912, she purchased a pie for each family seeking aid from the City Welfare Department, totaling 225. The Thanksgiving before saw 400 loaves of bread donated. In 1913, she commissioned a statue of Abraham Lincoln to be placed at the corner of State Street and Washington Street SE, also still there today. The day of dedication for the Longfellow bust also saw a magnificent fountain donated. Loraine stated that the fountain was memorializing her two boys, while Henry Wadsworth Longfellow was to honor Frederick. The quote Loraine chose

Fulton Street Park (Veterans Memorial Park) in the mid-1920s. *Grand Rapids City Archives and Records Center.*

of the poet's to be inscribed on his statue, meaningful for both the two boys and husband she had lost, was, "Life is real! Life is earnest! And the grave is not its goal."[2]

Longfellow's visage has endured in Veterans Memorial Park and stood witness as the city has changed over the years. Its patina betrays its age. The poet's words may not be widely remembered verbatim, but for Grand Rapids, Michigan, one passage of Longfellow's remains true. "For the structures that we raise, time is with materials filled; our to-days and yesterdays are the building blocks with which we build."[3]

Our present is built and informed by our past. As it is today, Grand Rapids does not exist without its history. Yesterday builds today. Much of that history is well known. The familiar stories of the logging and furniture industries dominate the popular narrative. While this aspect of the city's history is important, it is only half the story. It is the hidden history of the City of Grand Rapids that really informs its citizens why Grand Rapids is the way it is.

A NOTE ON SPELLING and terminology to keep in mind: when quoting directly, spelling and grammar are retained in their original form, even if the passages have misspellings, as in early diaries and communications. The terminology of the various city departments, commissions and councils can be confusing. The Village Board of Trustees, the Common Council and the City Commission all describe the city's leadership. The names changed over time, but the function remained the same. The terms used in the text correspond to the years citizens would have used them. For example, when discussing an ordinance in the 1890s, the Common Council voted on it. If they had passed the same law in the 1930s, it would have been the City Commission voting. Department names change over time, and the narrative attempts to relay that information in the text.

Chapter 1

Wood, Stone and Iron

O ak, elm and maple; ash and basswood; hickory and ironwood. Lands rolling; streams, marshes and swamps. From the foot of the rapids to their head, Lucius Lyon trekked across a relatively untamed river valley, describing the land he encountered: "To an Elm tree 10 in diameter fracl. cor. on Grand River. Land Rolling and 2nd rate. Timber oak. Church at Indian Village bears N 43 deg. W."[4]

In most narratives of the history of Grand Rapids, the story begins with the arrival of Louis Campau in 1826. Some narratives begin when Magdelaine La Framboise and her husband, Joseph, built an extensive fur-trading operation in the Grand River Valley before Campau's arrival. It also starts earlier with the Native Americans with whom they both traded.

This narrative, however, starts in 1931 when the federal survey system reached the Grand River Valley. Its roots can be quite literally measured to Michigan's neighbor Ohio. In Ohio, the geographer of the United States began surveying the American West. All the Midwest and beyond, survey by survey, was measured to that exact geographic point. It was in Cincinnati where the federal land offices operated. In Cincinnati, Lucius Lyon and other surveyors had to submit their hard-made measurements of what would become Grand Rapids.

Surveying work was painstakingly difficult. The labor required extensive knowledge of geometry. Nearly a decade after Lyon had surveyed this section of the Grand River, a young acquaintance asked for advice on becoming a surveyor. "You want patience, industry, and perseverance,"

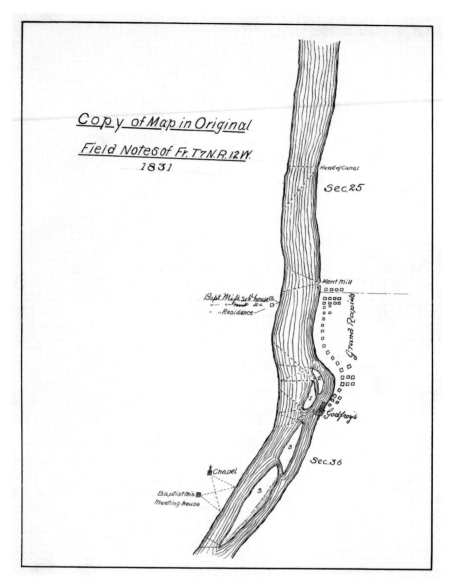

Lucius Lyon's 1831 sketch of the Grand River for his survey. *Grand Rapids City Archives and Records Center.*

Lyon responded. "By the time you get half done I presume you will be compelled to stop work on account of the mosquitos."[5] Even as late as 1935, a surveyor in the city engineers' office had trouble with mosquitos while working. He depicted the pest in his survey notebook, labeling its proboscis as dynamite.

Lyon, joined by a few assistants, worked long hours, from as soon as the sun rose until its final rays faded through the trees. They waded through the rough frontier of West Michigan, carrying their theodolites, compasses and measuring chains. Surveyors would use a triangulation process, in which a baseline was used, along with angles, to measure distances. Occasionally, they may have needed to erect small scaffolds to measure over impassable terrain. The government paid them by how many acres they surveyed, so the key was to survey in as few days as possible. "I never worked so hard in my life, and believe I never shall again," Lyon ended his advice.[6]

Lucius Lyon is a well-known figure in the city; his likeness stands in bronze in Lyon Square, at the end of Lyon Street. His contributions to Michigan are manifold, and his tenure as a senator has been written about extensively. Still, he and a handful of other men employed as surveyors provide

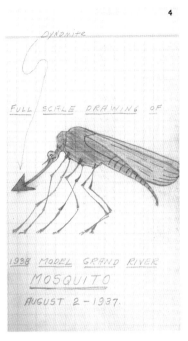

Page in the city engineer's survey journal from 1937 depicting the mosquitos tormenting surveyors. *Grand Rapids City Archives and Records Center.*

a unique window into early Grand Rapids. Surveyors, in general, occupy a particular but often overlooked chapter in the annals of American history. George Washington, Thomas Jefferson and Abraham Lincoln were all surveyors, as was the naturalist Henry David Thoreau. Meriwether Lewis and William Clark are more well known for their westward journey than their surveying prowess. John Almy and Wright Lewis Coffinberry are not household names in Grand Rapids. No street signs carry their names, at least not anymore. Yet Almy and Coffinberry were instrumental as early City of Grand Rapids surveyors.

THE SURVEYING SYSTEM STARTED with the passage of the Land Ordinance of 1785. The ordinance devised a plan whereby segments of land were divided into townships, each being six miles square. Each township was then divided into thirty-six sections. Sections 26, 25, 35 and 36 made up the land of early Grand Rapids. Sections were further divided into halves, quarters and beyond. Prospective settlers could then purchase specific sections, or fractions of sections, from the land offices, raising funds for a young government that had not yet been endowed with the authority to levy taxes.

The measuring of Grand Rapids began with John Mullett, surveyor general for all the Northwest Territories. Mullett was originally a tailor from Vermont but became well known for surveying large swaths of Michigan, including Mackinac Island. Mullett started his survey on February 1, 1831, measuring Sections 20 through 36 of Plainfield Township, the sections south of the Grand River. It took very little time to finish the survey, and the federal surveyor, General William Lytle, approved it in the land offices of Williamsburg, Ohio, less than seven days after Mullet started. Lytle operated the land office in Williamsburg, Ohio, at Harmony Hall, which has since transformed into a museum dedicated to preserving surveying history. Grand Rapids has a Harmony Hall restaurant, although the name-sharing is solely a coincidence.

After John Mullett surveyed near the Grand River, he moved southward, measuring the lands around Reeds Lake, then measured nearly all of Paris Township, as Kentwood used to be known. Two months later, Lucius Lyon began measuring the east side of the Grand River.

Lucius Lyon was a distinctive, unique man. He was five feet ten, with inquisitive gray eyes. His biographer described him as "very neat and particular in dress, rather slow in movement, impressive in bearing, courteous in manners, pleasant in voice, agreeable in conversation, especially with his acquaintances."[7] His letters, published by the Michigan Historical Commission, show a keen enthusiasm as he discusses business ventures, describes personal activities and composes poetry for his sister. Above all, he was a powerful advocate for Michigan. In 1822, he sent a letter to a man in Vermont arguing that while many "considered [Michigan] the waste land of the United States," he believed that "its situation for commerce is unrivalled" and that it "was found to possess an excellent soil."[8]

One key benefit to the surveying profession is that surveyors saw firsthand which lands were best suited for which business. They were often the first to see where stone might be quarried, where wood could best be milled and where land could best be tilled. Lyon saw that Grand Rapids was well suited for many ventures. Just four years after he surveyed the area, he and a partner paid excavators to dig a canal on the east side of the Grand River. Lyon invested in a new steamboat for the river. He also created the first salt well in Michigan at Grand Rapids.

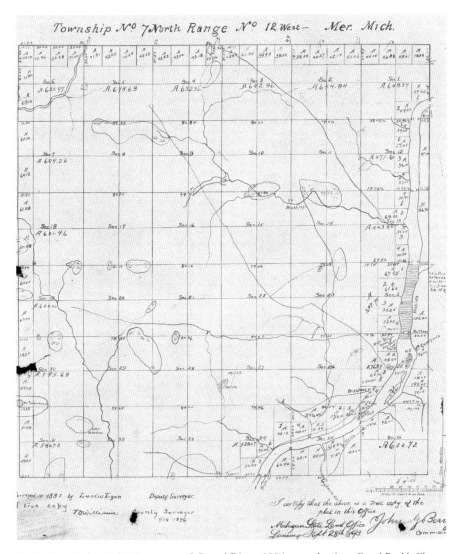

Lucius Lyon's detailed 1831 survey of Grand River; 1894 reproduction. *Grand Rapids City Archives and Records Center.*

During his first survey, Lyon undoubtedly came into contact with Louis Campau. Travelers and traders often stayed with Campau, or he would find lodging for them with his retinue, renting space to sleep or a table to eat. There were a handful of wooden cabins for a handful of French-speaking settlers; Campau was the only English speaker among them.

Campau and Lyon did not get along. In a letter Lyon wrote to Arthur Bronson in 1835, he described Campau as "a jealous, selfish and troublesome

Theodolite on display in the Grand Rapids City Engineer's Office. *Grand Rapids Engineering Department.*

Frenchman."[9] The two men could not have been more different. While Lyon was educated, neat and social, but aloof, Campau was rugged. He had only a scant education and was known for being short and gruff but also for his kindness and generosity. Sources confirmed that he did not particularly like the incoming Yankees.

The dislike was understandable. Campau's trading operation was successful. He enjoyed dealing with the Native Americans, often wearing clothes more akin to theirs than those of his fellow citizens. Campau likely knew that his trading operation would diminish the more settlers arrived. After surveyors submitted the Grand Rapids area section maps, Campau purchased the land he had already settled on, totaling seventy-two acres. Michigan Street bounded this area to the north, Fulton Street to the south, Division Avenue to the east and the river's edge to the west. The river's edge at that time would be today on the west side of Monroe Avenue below Pearl Street.

While Campau paid for the land in 1831, it was not until 1833 that he received his land patent from the General Land Offices at White Prairie. He organized his lands into lots to be sold, split by roads already present. Monroe Avenue, first used as an Indian trail, then adopted by Campau's trading post, ran at an angle. Nearly one year after Campau's land purchase, Lyon purchased his sections above and below Campau's.

The prevailing narrative has been that Lyon and Campau set up dueling villages, both angling to have theirs the dominant in the area, purposely platting them out to spite each other. The years have probably enhanced the feud beyond what it most likely was. Campau had his plat surveyed and mapped in 1833, selling the land between Pearl and Michigan Streets to Lucius Lyon to pay for the endeavor. It was not until 1836 that Lyon finalized his land's plat map. Lyon's correspondence and his early biography, published by the Michigan Pioneer and Historical Society, do not mention his Kent plat and give no mention of any troubles. Not only did he not mention street troubles, but he also discussed all his other business dealings in Kalamazoo and elsewhere, often in more detail than his Grand Rapids endeavors. Lucius Lyon likely had more pressing matters on his plate that required his attention. The connection issue from Canal to Monroe, often cited by historians, seems exaggerated. The 1836 plat of the Village of Kent and the plat of the Village of Grand Rapids show the passage open.

The street layout difference between the two proposed villages may have been born out of practicality more than spite. Prospect Hill—confusingly not located anywhere near Prospect Street—rose on the north side of

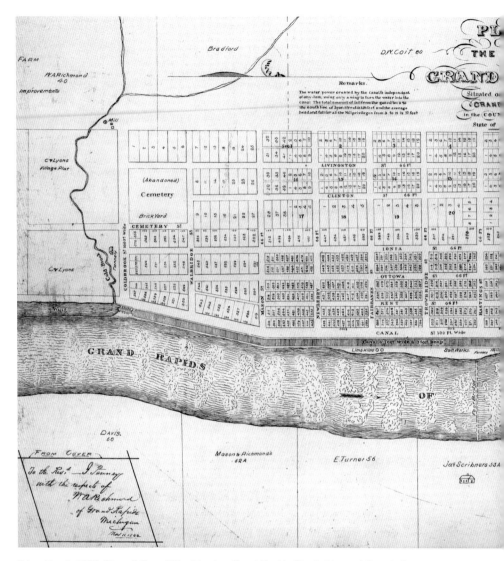

John Almy's 1836 City of Grand Rapids plat. *Grand Rapids City Archives and Records Center.*

Monroe sixty feet above the river level. In his *History of Grand Rapids*, Albert Baxter noted that the western portion of the hill on Monroe Center was very steep. A grid plat may have required extensive digging and grading of streets, which eventually did happen in the 1860s. As late as 1889, the dismantling of the hill was still ongoing.

That there were already several dwellings in the area also informed where streets could be laid out in Campau's plat, whereas by the time Lyon had

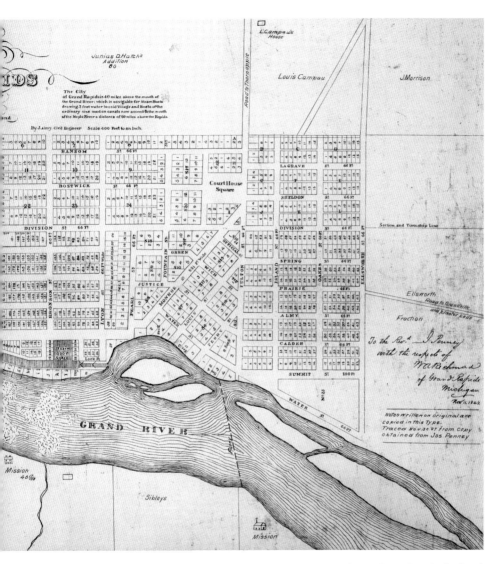

formed his plat, his land did not have as much activity. Despite their feud and its severity or lack thereof, the two men created the well-known layout of downtown Grand Rapids. It was another surveyor, however, who mapped downtown Grand Rapids.

JOHN ALMY WAS BORN just outside of Boston in the 1790s. His father was also named John, which made him a junior, but no sources refer to him as such. He traveled to Grand Rapids in 1835 by way of Detroit. He and his wife stayed the first night with Louis Campau. In a short time, Almy became instrumental in shaping early Grand Rapids.

Almy created survey maps for Lyon and, using Charles Barnes's survey for Campau's village plat, completed the final map of the incorporated Village of Grand Rapids in 1936. Almy had assistance in the endeavor from John W. Pierce, his wife's brother, who opened a bookstore in Grand Rapids, the first in the state outside of Detroit. The year after having mapped out the streets and the lots of the village, Almy was elected as the second state representative to serve his district, which at that time included Kent, Ottawa, Clinton and Ionia Counties.

John Almy.

Portrait of John Almy. *Memorials of the Grand River Valley.*

Even while a state representative, Almy continued his surveying work, staking out prospective projects around the state for the legislature. In 1837, he surveyed a potential ship canal around the Sault Ste. Marie, under the direction of Governor Stevens T. Mason, and around the same time, the busy surveyor platted a prospective town called Superior, now the Waukazoo Woods neighborhood in Park Township. He also was in charge of proposing and mapping improvements to the Grand and Kalamazoo Rivers.

Despite traveling throughout the state, John Almy knew his home was Grand Rapids. In 1839, he built a modest house for his family, the first stone residence in Grand Rapids. Long gone now, the house would have stood roughly where the Kent County Office building is now.

After Almy left the state legislature, he became an associate judge for Kent County. Many correspondents and contemporaries referred to their friend solely as Judge Almy, even after his term ended in 1841. Despite Almy's prolific career, many sources do not delve much into his history. One reason for this may be due to a devastating fire that in 1860 destroyed much of the early records of Kent County.

The man was immensely busy, focusing on many endeavors—attorney, surveyor, engineer, representative, judge. While Almy was judge, he simultaneously served as the president of the Grand River Bank, the first bank in the city. Lucius Lyon also served as a member of the bank's board. Coincidentally, while Almy was a representative, he was one of four legislators who voted against a wildcat banking bill.

John Almy, like Lucius Lyon, was a stalwart proponent of Michigan and Grand Rapids. Newly elected governor John Barry appointed John Almy as an immigration agent in 1845. John Almy had already organized a network of contacts promoting Michigan, specifically Grand Rapids, between Michigan and New York. Almy had to reside in New York for a time to lure potential settlers. While there, he published a booklet titled *State of Michigan—1845—To Emigrants*, in both English and German.

In his publication, Almy enticingly described the Grand River area. "In the valley, and on the banks of this River, are some of the finest Lands in the State." Almy wrote that there were many principal towns on the river; "Grand Rapids however, is the important point."[10] Almy explained how potential immigrants could purchase land at $1.25 per acre or go through state warrants and pay $0.70 per acre. Almy described the village he had mapped out not ten years prior and all the industries in the village, most likely so that a prospective immigrant would know what would be available and what would be needed that he could supply. Almy wrote that in 1845 there were

> *Fifteen stores, Three flour mills, Two saw mills, Two furnaces and machine shops, Two pail factories, Two tanneries, One woolen factory, One sash factory, salt works, plaster mill, two hatters, three shoe shops, Three tailors, one tin and coppersmith, One saddler, several blacksmiths, Three public houses, Two printing offices, Four churches, One incorporated academy, and Four physicians.*[11]

ALMY THEN NOTED HOW to visit Grand Rapids and how new residents could send their belongings to the village, either traversing the road from Detroit to Battle Creek and on to the settlement or passing through the Great Lakes and up the Grand River by steamboat. Martin Hendricks, a recent immigrant from the Netherlands, traveled to Grand Rapids in 1847; he became a carpenter and served the city as a tax collector for a time. Hendricks cited Almy's pamphlet as his reason for coming to the Grand River Valley.

After John Almy returned to Grand Rapids, the village was growing and on the verge of becoming a full-fledged city. Once incorporated, the city hired Almy as city surveyor for a time, though he was not the first city surveyor.

On a brisk day in early May 1855, Wright Lewis Coffinberry hired a horse and buggy from in town. He had packed his surveying equipment and visited a furnace owned by Daniel Ball, where he would occasionally engineer his tools. Coffinberry took from the forge a bundle of iron stakes he had crafted and met with A.C. McKenzie, a twenty-year-old surveying assistant. Coffinberry and McKenzie rode through the city in their horse and buggy, placing stakes into the ground at every section and one-fourth section corners of the city.

The first few days in May were only the beginning of the project. It took until July to set all the stakes, sometimes replacing wood stakes with iron if they came across remnants of an old surveyor's work. Coffinberry produced two maps depicting the staking work he and his young assistant produced. The maps noted where they identified and placed the wood, stone and iron stakes. In his autobiography many years later, Coffinberry wrote that he was immensely proud of this specific project.

Grand Rapids adopted a city charter in 1850, dividing the city into five wards. Moving toward more systematic planning, platting and grading of the city, the alderman swore in Wright Lewis Coffinberry as city surveyor the same year. The position was more akin to that of a municipal engineer, providing any land work the community needed. Coffinberry staked out lots and plats for residents and set the grades and widths of streets, following up with assessments for financing the projects. Coffinberry enjoyed the work, was scientifically curious and was generally well respected in the community.

Coffinberry's father, George, whose native German name was Kauffenbaerger, was born in 1760 in Virginia before the Revolutionary War and proceeded to fight against the British when he was sixteen. Near the end of the eighteenth century, George Coffinberry moved his family to Ohio, where Wright was born. Wright distinctly remembered the War of 1812, and his rudimentary village of thirteen families was at the forefront of the troubles. In his autobiography, he recounted a memory in which a passing soldier saw him sitting with a toy drum, plucked him up and placed him on his shoulder, taking him into the army camp to entertain the troops.

Life on the frontier was often precarious. Coffinberry married Jane Beach in 1831, though the marriage may have been out of necessity, for one month later, their first daughter, Eunice, was born. Coffinberry had lost four brothers earlier in their family's history, and Eunice died ten years after she was born. Coffinberry mentions neither his daughter's birth nor her death in his autobiography. He was writing some forty years after the fact, but it speaks of the silent suffering of the time.

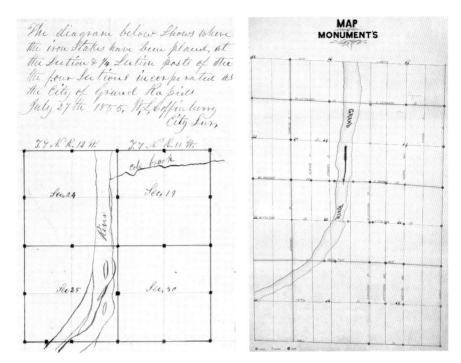

Left: Sketch of Grand Rapids sections by Wright L. Coffinberry from 1855. *Grand Rapids City Archives and Records Center.*

Right: Map of monuments, showing wood, stone and iron stakes set in sections within the city in 1855. *Grand Rapids City Archives and Records Center.*

Coffinberry moved his wife and four other children to Michigan in the 1840s. Two of his brothers had already moved to the Saint Joseph area. Coffinberry and Jane first settled in Centerville but found it was not growing as fast as they liked. They moved in June 1846 to Grand Rapids. Coffinberry noted in his autobiography that when he arrived, "I noticed the rapids in the river, I noticed the magnificent water power which the rapids afforded, the gypsum beds in the immediate vicinity, the manufacture of salt, with pine timber in almost inexhaustible quantities easy of access, while the soil was of fair quality for agricultural purposes" Coffinberry prophesized that someday, "I might see a city of a hundred thousand population in this place."[12]

The city at the time was growing. The hardships of the late 1830s were over, and the population was increasing, likely due to Almy's advertising efforts. Coffinberry noted that there were roughly two thousand inhabitants when he arrived and that half of that number were Native Americans.

Coffinberry was elected city surveyor a few months after the city incorporated. As the new city grew, citizens put Coffinberry to work. A small number of Coffinberry's early city records are held in the Grand Rapids City Archives; only some of his engineering drawings survived. Despite this, his city records and his papers stored at the Bentley Historical Library at the University of Michigan provide detailed information about early Grand Rapids and his surveying work, the work of organizing the physical layout of Grand Rapids.

Coffinberry's first year of work was surprisingly slow. The Common Council fixed his salary at two dollars a day. He noted in his autobiography that he made only fifty dollars in his first year of work. It also must be pointed out that he and his assistants could only accomplish the bulk of their work in fair weather. In July 1850, less than one month after starting, Coffinberry submitted his plan for the grade of streets, showing the slopes of streets. His work focused mainly on physically measuring and organizing streets and staking out lots for residents.

Coffinberry operated a watch repair shop that functioned more as a general engineering shop to furnish his remaining necessary income. It sat on the southwest corner of Monroe Center and Ottawa Avenue, the later site of Herpolsheimer's and the current location of the Grand Rapids Art Museum. Coffinberry was a talented engineer. He often crafted surveying instruments for himself and other surveyors in town.

In the spring of 1855, snow was still covering the ground, which may have put Coffinberry in a poor mood. In a rare fit of complaints, he

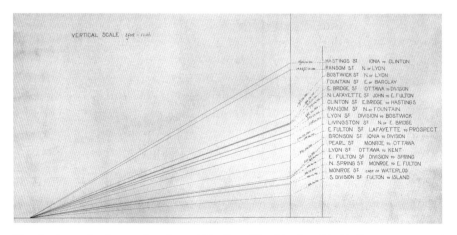

Plan for the grade of street elevations within Grand Rapids. *Grand Rapids City Archives and Records Center.*

described the jeweler's profession as "one of the meanest kinds of business that ever a man was plagued with." Despite being kept busy by his shop, he resented much of his work. He despised repairing jewelry and mending baubles for people. "Melvina must have her fine gold chain mended, for St. Marks is a fashionable church and it would appear very vulgar to be there without the gold fixings," he wrote wryly in 1855.[13] He much preferred his surveying work.

After his first year as city surveyor, Coffinberry had established a solid reputation, which led to him acquiring a few state contracts to survey around Michigan, going as far as the Grand Traverse Bay area. In 1854, he returned to surveying work for Grand Rapids. As mentioned previously, the surveying was confined to spring, summer and fall. Winter months were filled with long days working in the shop. In the winter, sleigh legs replaced the wheels of wagons, but surveying was more difficult in the snow, if not impossible.

Once the thaw came with a new year, residents kept Coffinberry busy. His daily journal became filled with small surveying and engineering projects around the city. He drew profiles of streets, such as he did in late March 1855 for College Avenue and Sheldon Street. He mapped out street grades and did the work of leveling roads to match the assigned grade, as he did for Lyon street in May 1855. Residents had him survey lots for them. On April 3, he surveyed three lots for Christoph Kusterer, one of the first brewers in the city.

While Coffinberry kept his work life busy, his diary also details his personal life. He attended scientific lectures and often wrote about his own scientific interests and theories. He and his wife entertained guests, many of them speakers from outside the city, who often stayed with his family or at least dined with them during their visits. He and his wife attended the concerts at John W. Pierce's hall or went to St. Marks to hear a choir performance.

One of the more clandestine activities Coffinberry partook in, however, was séances. He and other early city residents would gather together and attempt to make contact with souls beyond the veil. One of the members would relay that they indeed were channeling a spirit, and the others would pepper them with questions. In the spring of 1855, Coffinberry wrote about one such séance, a channeling of a spirit that predicted death.

It was a small social gathering on a clear, cold night. A few friends had come over to the Coffinberry residence. Sitting in the living room, lit only by candles, for dusk had settled upon the group, a séance began. One of the host's friends, a Mr. Wyman, relayed that a spirit had made contact and taken control of him as a conduit to the unearthly realm. Wyman

Grand Rapids city surveyors measuring the widths of roads in 1931. *Grand Rapids City Archives and Records Center.*

relayed that the ghost of Napoleon Bonaparte of France, dead since 1821, was speaking through him from the world beyond. The spirit had some news of great importance: the Emperor of Russia, Nicholas I, was going to be assassinated soon, and the country of Poland, under Russia's rule, would subsequently be freed. Coincidentally or not, just a few weeks later, Nicholas I died of pneumonia.

SURVEYORS LIKE LUCIUS LYON, John Almy and Wright Lewis Coffinberry influenced the layout of Grand Rapids. Author Robert Greene states, "Human nature ends up shaping what we create." These three surveyors infused their natures into the streets and lots of the city they abstractly created through their work. Coffinberry was responsible for many of the minute details of the face of Grand Rapids. He calculated the grades of streets and the widths of curbs. All the while, he attended séances, enjoyed time with his family and was a member and part of the community. To some degree, the city is an expression of Coffinberry's, just like it is an expression

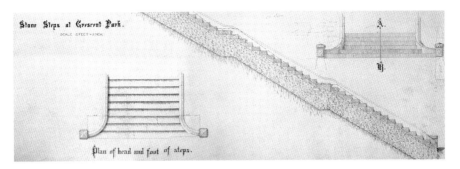

Stone Steps at Crescent Park.
SCALE 4 FEET = 1 INCH

Plan of head and foot of steps.

Blueprint for the stone steps in Crescent Park, built in the 1860s or 1870s. *Grand Rapids City Archives and Records Center.*

of us all. We instill a part of ourselves in our work, and Coffinberry instilled much of his life in the city.

The city surveyor's position and staff officially became the city's Engineering Department in 1888. The civil engineers, often hunched over their drafting tables, were artists in their own right. They created beautiful, intricate drawings of all aspects of the city: public buildings and parks; bridges, dams and great machines of engineering precision; streets that run through the city like veins; curbs and sidewalks; plazas; sewers; and grand projects like the Civic Auditorium. They translated engineering into placemaking, crafting a beautiful city. One perfect example is a drawing of the stairs at Crescent Park. Coffinberry drew the proposed set of fifty-six steps leading up the hill of Crescent Park. The plan is undated, but Francis H. Cumings donated the land in 1858, and the park was regraded in the 1860s. Nearly every physical public place in the city can trace its lineage to the Engineering Department and its early city surveyors.

CHAPTER 2

FOR HUMANITY'S SAKE

On a chilly, dry afternoon after an early dinner on May 18, 1855, Wright Lewis Coffinberry was joined on Sheldon Avenue SE by Alderman William N. Cook. The two men had gathered, carrying their surveying equipment to measure the width of the street.

Alderman Cook was also a member of one of the first firefighting organizations, Alert Fire Company No. 1. He moved to the city in 1843 and opened and operated a prominent blacksmith shop, becoming a supplier for much of the community. Albert Baxter noted that the sign of his shop included the quote "The Hope of Reward Sweetens Labor."[14]

Cook helped Coffinberry measure Sheldon Avenue SE because property owners and residents on Sheldon had petitioned the Common Council, on which Cook sat, to fix an error in the plat. Coffinberry and Cook located the old wooden stakes and found that Sheldon, LaGrave and Jefferson Avenues skewed eastward. The lots between Elm and Wealthy Streets were twenty feet deeper than those four blocks to the north. Sheldon angled east when it instead should have been parallel with Division Avenue.

The plat, setting out the widths and lengths of lots, was created by Edmund B. Bostwick, for which a street is named. Bostwick was an early resident, arriving in 1837. By 1855, when residents realized he had incorrectly platted his addition to the city, Bostwick had already passed away. He had left the growing city in 1850 for California and warmer climes but died in the Rocky Mountains.

Residents petitioned to fix the plat by shortening Sheldon to sixty-six feet instead of the existing eighty-six feet. Most likely, residents had not realized

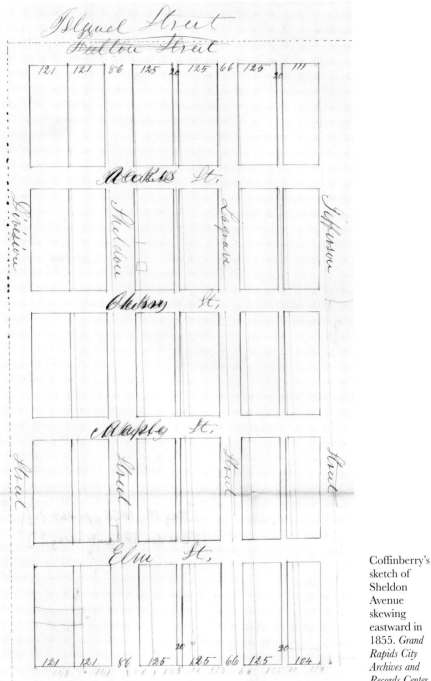

Coffinberry's sketch of Sheldon Avenue skewing eastward in 1855. *Grand Rapids City Archives and Records Center.*

where lots were and had built structures into the rudimentary road. The street was not graded and improved until 1858. This occurrence was far more common before the city added curbs and paved streets. In the 1880s, a big project arose in which city engineers attempted to fix streets that had buildings or fences encroaching into the road.

The men who petitioned were not the most prominent—most don't receive detailed biographies in Baxter's *History of Grand Rapids*—but they, like many other early citizens, drove changes within the community: men like John Stowell, a carpenter who lived with his wife on the street and owned two lots, or Thomas Berry, a mason who lived on Sheldon between Oakes and Cherry and owned two lots. The most prominent residents on the petition were Francis H. Cuming, William H. McConnell and John M. Smith. The three men held over half of the eighty-two lots represented on the petition. Francis H. Cuming was the only one of the group who was prominent enough to warrant a full extended biography. He is probably most well known today for being the driving factor behind Crescent Park. William H. McConnell had been overshadowed in the narrative by his brother John. Henry Bremer, another signer of the petition, actually has his photo in Baxter's *History* but only a short biography. Hiram Hinsdill, another signer, served as a village trustee, and many village board meetings convened at his house. He is mentioned briefly as the builder of the National Hotel, a precursor to the Morton House.

The lot owners wanted the plat fixed by shortening Sheldon Avenue so they could retain their larger lot sizes. Owners had already built cabins, homes and fences to some degree, and residents did not want to move buildings. Coffinberry's report, however, submitted to the Common Council, was that the original plat maker intended the southernmost lots to be uniform with the northernmost lots. The south lots would be reduced from 141 feet to 121 feet, correcting the original error. Coffinberry had brought Alderman Cook along on the survey of Sheldon in part to bear witness to the error. He likely knew the ire it would draw from the lot owners.

The Committee on Streets reported to the Common Council that the city had no legal standing to take twenty feet from the road to give to property owners. The only legal recourse to fix the plat was to correct the larger lots.

The neighborhood has changed significantly; no longer do any single-family homes rest on the street. The Ladies Literary Club is the last remnant of the notion that the avenue was at one point residential, and even that was built over thirty years after the lots changed.

Petition submitted to the Common Council by Sheldon Avenue residents asking the council to fix the street lines in 1855. *Grand Rapids City Archives and Records Center.*

Mark Twain wrote, "History never repeats itself, but the kaleidoscopic combinations of the pictures present often seem to be constructed out of the broken fragments of antique legends."[15] Often, this is shortened to "History never repeats itself, but it rhymes." In 1915, property owners again petitioned the city regarding Sheldon Avenue. This time they requested the city not repave the street. City commissioner Elvin Swarthout received much of the ire from letter writers and petitioners because he had brought up the resolution for repaving.

Elvin Swarthout, bespectacled and highly educated, served on the Common Council and the City Commission. He also served on the Board of Education and was instrumental in fundraising for the Charles Belknap statue in Belknap Park. Swarthout had his hand in numerous city projects and served as mayor twice. He practiced law in the city and volunteered as the Grand Rapids Boy Scouts Council president.

Residents petitioned that the repaving was unnecessary and that simply repairing the road would suffice. The cost of repairs was also a reason they did not want the city to repave the road; they did not have the funds. Residents may have still been struggling after a short economic depression in 1913 and 1914. Saint Andrews Church, the Ladies Literary Club and the All Souls Church signed the petition, along with forty-four others, most of whom were homeowners, as the street was still heavily residential.

Unlike the first petition in the 1850s, this petition came at a time when public norms were changing, and women joined the ranks of signers. Again, many of the signers were not as prominent as other members of the Grand Rapids society at the time, but they were hardworking and essential to the city's functioning. Women like Clara Woodcock, who lived at 321 Sheldon Avenue SE, roughly where the entrance to Catholic Central High School is, signed. Clara worked at Globe Knitting Works and eventually became a hand screw operator at the Metal Parts Manufacturing Company. Three years later, Clara signed up for war work with the Council of National Defense.

Nora Crahen also signed the petition. J. Boyd Pantlind employed her as a bookkeeper at the Pantlind Hotel. She also signed up for war work three years later and listed Pantlind as her reference. However, Nora was in poor health and would pass away five years after signing the petition.

Mother and daughter Emma B. Winegar and Alice W. Tinkham signed the petition, as well. Emma's husband, William, had passed away in 1904. Alice lived at 361 Sheldon, a home at the corner of Sheldon and Wealthy, a corner that no longer exists. Alice had lived there for many years and hosted many local social gatherings. Alice eventually joined the League of Women Voters and participated in campaigning throughout 1921.

Signers of the petition were vindicated when the city capitulated and went to work repairing the street instead of repaving it. Sheldon was eventually repaved in 1917, two years after a quick repair job; bricks were discarded, and asphalt was used. The condition of Sheldon, from its lot size deviations to the repaving of its road, can be interesting if you know the street. The real story surrounds the people: those who lived on the street, those petitioning the city for changes and the city leaders and workers who responded.

As the chapter title suggests, this section revolves around humanity. As much as Grand Rapids is the main character in its own history, its people are the drivers of that history. Cities are "humanity inscribed on the face of the earth," to steal a phrase from Henry David Thoreau.[16] The people of Grand Rapids cannot be divorced from any aspect of the city's history. The hidden facets of Grand Rapids's history are informed by the people living in the city.

FROM ITS BEGINNING, GRAND Rapids has been formed by those who immigrated to its valley. Descent, or nationality, was central to individuals in the city's early days. Neighborhoods were populated mainly by one demographic. English, Irish, German and Dutch built homes near those they could most easily relate to and communicate with. Descent is still significant, though its influence on the city lessens over the years. Despite this, the resonance of its past importance can still be found.

The city was originally a French trading post, but French influences today are not self-evident. From 1826 to 1833, the primary language spoken by settlers was French. Some street names carry French names, such as Campau and Lafayette. Some buildings in Grand Rapids once sported French influence as well. Local historian Thomas R. Dilley, in an essay on an architectural style known as the French Second Empire, noted that all buildings in Grand Rapids built in that style were eventually torn down. Dilley's example of the Clark mansion was the norm: it sported a French mansard roofline with dormer windows. While the French population initially outnumbered the incoming settlers, they were soon overwhelmed. By 1880, of the roughly seventy thousand inhabitants of Kent County, only sixty individuals were French.

The largest share of early settlers immigrated from the northeastern United States. New Englanders and New Yorkers arrived with their families and traditions. A contingent of Irish laborers came to work on Lucius Lyon's canal in the mid-1830s. Once John Almy and Edmund Bostwick started the business of promoting immigration to the Grand River Valley, an influx of individuals, mostly of German and Dutch descent, moved into the city. Baxter wrote in *History of Grand Rapids* that in 1849, the newspapers claimed, "Our streets have been 'taken by the Dutch.'"[17]

Immigration was central to Grand Rapids's early growth. Baxter wrote that a steady stream of Dutch, Irish and German peoples sought to make this city their home. Industry was at the forefront of enticing immigrants to fill their labor needs. Baxter also noted that as late as 1871, the Grand Rapids and Indiana Railroad Company sent an emissary to Scandinavian countries to convince their people to immigrate to the area. A slight string of Polish immigrants came to Grand Rapids in 1855, but a considerable number arrived during the 1870s to work in the furniture industries. Baxter's *History of Grand Rapids* was published in 1891. In his chapter on immigration, he noted that there was no longer a need to advertise or form organizations to promote immigration. Families encouraged immigration through their networks, and Grand Rapids was also able to grow naturally from within.

EVENTUALLY, ANIMOSITY AROSE AGAINST the immigrants coming into the city. It originated in struggles over labor. A depression started in 1882 and lasted for three years. Wages were stagnant, and work was hard to come by. The common fear the newspapers wrote of was that immigrants would fill positions that settled citizens of the city desperately needed. Organizations popped up to promote anti-immigration sentiments. Norton Smith resided on the northeast side of town in 1895 and attempted to organize a chapter of the Knights of Protection. This anti-immigration organization restricted its membership to white male citizens.

The anti-immigration sentiments that broke through the community, to a large extent, focused on Chinese immigrants. In 1888, the U.S. senator from Grand Rapids, Melbourne H. Ford, wrote a letter to the Reverend Simon Ponganis of St. Adelbert's Church. Ponganis had publicly expressed concern that the Committee on Immigration in Congress was proposing to restrict all types of immigration. He was explicitly worried that Polish immigrants, which most of his parishioners were, would be banned from entering the country. Ford wrote back and published the transcript in the *Evening Leader* newspaper. The committee "has never in any instance taken any action in regard to the exclusion of any particular nationality or people except the Chinese."[18] In 1882, Congress passed the Chinese Exclusion Act, which prohibited Chinese individuals from immigrating to the country and receiving citizenship. The act would expire in ten years, and the legislature renewed it in 1892 for the same duration. In 1902, Congress again renewed it, this time without an expiration date.

Grand Rapids had a small Chinese population. The city may have been the location, in 1874, of the first naturalization of a Chinese immigrant, that of a well-known Chinese man named Wong Chin Foo. The Grand Rapids Historical Commission wrote a short article on Foo, relaying that he had been lecturing in the city when he decided to apply for citizenship there. A 1902 *Grand Rapids Herald* article noted that the city boasted thirty Chinese residents, the most prominent of which was Chan Hoy.

Chan Hoy was born in China in 1864 and immigrated to America in 1880. He opted to come alone. Hoy eventually moved to Grand Rapids in the mid-1880s, returning only once to China to father a son with his wife. It appears he worked odd jobs until he could start an importing business, shipping goods from China and selling them as novelties. He eventually opened a restaurant and two laundromats in the city. The press labeled him the "King of Chinatown."[19] Hoy was fighting an uphill battle. The local trade organizations attempted to ruin his business. In 1900, the Trades and Labor Council passed a resolution to ban members from being patrons of any laundromats that Chinese proprietors ran.

Chop Suey, Chan Hoy's Chinese restaurant. *Grand Rapids Public Museum.*

Chinese immigrants also had their supporters, such as Julius C. Burrows, a senator from Michigan. The Grand Rapids Historical Commission noted that when in 1899, the Carvers Union in the city passed a resolution to boycott Chinese laundromats, one member stood up against the resolution, stating that he would still be using the laundromats because of their superb service.

In 1902, Hoy started planning for the education of his son, Chan Sing, planning on having the boy join him in Grand Rapids. Hoy prepared all the necessary paperwork and applied for his son to immigrate. His success or failure hinged on the requirements of the Chinese Exclusion Act. A merchant already established in the United States could bring family members to join him, so Hoy had to prove he was a merchant. It was lucky that Hoy had also started to run a grocery store on Bridge Street, because the law did not count restaurateurs or laundromat owners as merchants. Unfortunately, E.H. Tippert, the immigration investigator in Michigan, decided that because Hoy owned multiple businesses, he was not a full-time merchant and thus denied his son's entry. After a lengthy appeal, Tippert returned and spent time photographing Hoy's grocery store and conducting interviews about Hoy around town. Tippert reluctantly approved the request, and Chan Sing departed Hong Kong. When leaving Hong Kong, Chan Sing was required to pay fifty dollars to cure a "diseased eye" malady that a port official fraudulently diagnosed to extort the young man.

Once Sing arrived in San Francisco, he had another dubious bout of "diseased eye," and officials turned him away. Hoy and those helping him attempted to appeal yet again. The clerk of the Bureau of Immigration reviewed the files and asserted that the accounts of bribery in Hong Kong and San Francisco were false. The clerk questioned the boy's paternity and moved to deny a *Grand Rapids Press* reporter access to Sing's file. Sing was eventually able to enter the country and moved to Grand Rapids to be with his father. In 1910, Sing took a trip to visit his mother back in China. Instead of San Francisco, he decided to try his luck going through Canada and attempted to enter the United States at Portal, North Dakota.

However, Sing encountered more problems there. An immigration agent made a data entry error, listing Sing as far older than he was. When his papers showed that he was on his way back to his father in Grand Rapids, authorities detained him. Chan Hoy worked with Senator Julius C. Burrows to plead his case in the country's capital. The *Grand Rapids Press* noted that Hoy's reputation as a wealthy businessman saved his son from being turned away again. One article claimed authorities called a dentist to check

Application for restaurant license filled out by Chan Hoy in 1908. *Grand Rapids City Archives and Records Center.*

the youth's teeth to determine his correct age. Eventually, father and son reunited in Grand Rapids.

Chan Hoy's restaurant Chop Suey, located at the corner of Monroe and Pearl, was a Grand Rapids favorite. When the restaurant closed briefly in 1908 over a licensing problem, the *Grand Rapids Press* called it a "dire event" and assuaged readers' fears with a guarantee that their favorite Chinese restaurant would soon be open again.[20] Applicants for a restaurant license had to garner the signatures of community members attesting to their good standing in the city. Hoy had applied for his license in April, and as a testament to his standing in the community, city clerk John Boer was the first to sign for Hoy.

Other signatories included Dr. Alden Williams, a bacteriologist who would later become the official radiologist for the city in 1915. Williams's building sat across the street from Chop Suey, and Williams likely ordered frequently. E.M. McCoy, a doctor who also had his practice on Monroe Avenue, was the last to sign the document. All signers were likely patrons of Hoy's restaurant.

As the "king" of Grand Rapids's Chinatown, Chan Hoy also had to deal with rivals and other Chinese immigrants attempting to usurp his crown. He complained to the *Grand Rapids Press* that a rival restaurant would call and place fake orders, wasting Chop Suey's time and resources delivering mouthwatering food to unsuspecting houses throughout the town. On one occasion, a newly arrived Chinese immigrant named Ma Fo Mooney approached Hoy and claimed he was a secret service agent with the U.S. Treasury Department, demanding sixty dollars from Hoy. Hoy did not relinquish the payment and instead had the man arrested for fraud. Mooney's mug shot resides in the Grand Rapids Public Museum's collection.

Police records, in general, provide a fascinating and rare look into nationalities. The mug shot collections within the Grand Rapids City Archives and Records Center and the Grand Rapids Public Museum provide details on members of society often overlooked by traditional historical accounts.

While acknowledging that the individuals represented in criminal records are often victims of economic and social systems, many acting out of desperation, ignorance or both, the stories within are humanizing and

Mug shot of Ma Fo Mooney, who attempted to defraud Chan Hoy. *Grand Rapids Public Museum.*

personal. There are only two instances in the 1928–34 mug shot book in the city archives in which the offense provided is "violation of immigration law."

The two men, Fung Linn and Choy Linn, were well-dressed, sporting ties and short black hair. They were arrested on May 4 at 122 Monroe and deported the following month. Grand Rapids seemed to take no notice of the occurrence, for the *Grand Rapids Press* was silent. Who were these two men? They may have come to the country in search of prosperity, driven by the intrinsically human need to provide for one's own, to carve out a piece of the world to call one's own. They may have fled China due to Japan's invasion of Manchuria. The images of the two men may be the only photographs of them that have survived, preserving a small aspect of their life stories.

President Franklin D. Roosevelt eventually repealed the Chinese Exclusion Act in 1943. Chinese immigrants were finally able to become citizens once more. A Rockford man named Dor Yen became the first in Kent County to apply for citizenship.

Chinese immigrants, however, were not the only ones who faced hardships in an adoptive country.

STONES FLEW AT THE heads of six Polish students, hurled by twelve Polish women. Charges of sympathizing with the Kaiser and the German army in Europe were flung along with the stones. The altercation happened on a Friday night on Division Avenue, in the shadow of St. Isidore's steeples. The students had recently left the church organization and joined what was informally called the Russell sect. The International Bible Students' association espoused a pacifist message; the students had been handing its pamphlets out. While one student's head needed heavy bandages after the stoning, the special agent of the U.S. Department of Justice, William S. Fitch, recommended that the court prosecute the six for disorderly conduct.

Fitch had spent his early career as a Secret Service agent after graduating from Georgetown University with degrees in law. Before the war broke out in Europe, Fitch was already working with the American Protection League around Milwaukee and Chicago. When America joined its overseas allies, his position primed him for advancement to become a special agent for the Justice Department.

During World War I, fear descended on the country like a plague—fear that German Americans would rise and fight for their home country within their adoptive one. Men like Carl Wilhelm Muller, charged with vagrancy and sent to the county jail, were sent to internment camps to wait out the conflict or until they were proven not to sympathize with the opposition. Some cases of sedition may have confirmed the fear to be well founded, but most were likely born solely of misunderstanding. Muller had served in the German army before immigrating to this country, and the press claimed he had lost five brothers killed in battle.

Wilhelm Seeger wrote an article for the *Grand River Valley Magazine* of the Grand Rapids Historical Society documenting German American history in Grand Rapids. He noted that the Grand Rapids Public Library removed many German language periodicals from its collection. Grand Rapids public schools stopped teaching German, and schools rid their libraries and curriculums of materials that they felt painted Germans in a favorable light.

One such case was that of James Harvey Robinson's *Medieval and Modern Times*. Robinson was an American historian whose ancestors immigrated to New England in the mid-1600s from the Netherlands. He released his new edition of *Medieval and Modern Times* in 1916. An attorney alerted Agent Fitch, who labeled it as "insidious German propaganda." He claimed the new edition had changes that highlighted German history, a veiled "attempt to break down sentiment in favor of the allied nations and to strengthen sentiment in favor of German military domination."[21]

On Monday, February 4, 1918, all German and Austrian men were required to report to the police headquarters and submit their application to register as an "alien enemy." This measure would allow them to continue as they had before the United States entered the war. If they failed to submit their application by February 9, authorities would force them to wait out the war in an internment camp, like Muller. German women were not yet required to register, but the *Grand Rapids Press* noted that women suspected of harboring anti-war sentiments "will be dealt with the same as men."[22]

Some German Americans were horrified to learn that they were not citizens when immigration agents came calling. Fathers who had meant to file naturalization paperwork but put it off put their children in a bind. Marriages also complicated matters. Mary, born in Grand Rapids, became an "alien enemy" because she had married a German man by the name of Paul Gutzeit. The Expatriation Act of 1907 put into law a precedent adhered to throughout the preceding century. The citizenship of women depended on the citizenship of their husbands. Married women could also not seek their own citizenship and had to rely on their husbands to file for citizenship. This misogynistic practice would be heavily fought against in the 1920s by waves of women exercising their new voting powers. The

Kusterer Brewing Company, circa 1890. *Grand Rapids Public Museum.*

Grand Rapids Press, which usually wrote in a tone suggesting approval of anti-German practices, threw its weight behind Mary Gutzeit. It noted the cruel irony that Mary was labeled a foreign enemy when her father had fought valiantly for the Union during the Civil War directly under Ulysses S. Grant. Just three days before she was required to register as an enemy of the state, Mary had enlisted to help the war effort with the Women's National Defense Committee.

For his Grand Rapids Historical Society article on German American history, Wilhelm Seeger noted that the anti-German sentiments that wound their way through Grand Rapids marked the end of a prominent German community within Grand Rapids. Perhaps some sought to downplay their heritage, as German clubs and organizations ceased to gather in the 1920s. Few German influences are evident today within the city, but they are there if you know where to look. Just recently, David Ringler, owner of Cedar Springs Brewing Company, opened a "Munich-style" beer hall in Grand Rapids. The beer hall's name, Kusterer Brauhaus, echoes history, honoring the early German brewer Christoph Kusterer, who came to Grand Rapids in 1844.

THE HUMAN ELEMENT IN Grand Rapids drives the lion's share of the city's history. Community members, civic leaders, neighbors and workers steer every city project. Every business is managed, to some degree, and patronized by community members. The human element can drive things as minor as the repaving of streets or as monumental as how people treat each other within the city.

Todd R. Robinson documented the history of the African American civil rights movement in Grand Rapids in his book *A City within a City*. The book is a prime example of the experience of a group of community members interacting and having interactions forced on them by other community members. There may seem like no connection between the paving of Sheldon Avenue and the treatment of an ethnic group. The stakes are drastically, painfully different. However, both are driven by interactions within and throughout the community. Humanity is intrinsically linked, by minor occurrences in the city as much as by monumental social interactions.

In 1917, the newly organized Grand Rapids Red Cross unveiled a new campaign, the same month that the United States entered World War I. The need for nurses and volunteers to care for wounded soldiers was rising, and the need was growing locally as well; the Red Cross desperately needed funds and volunteers. One *Grand Rapids Press* article stated that only one third of the wounded had adequate care. The organization adhered to a neutral position, serving the hurt of all nations. They needed their new slogan to "ring from one end of Grand Rapids to the other."[23] The slogan was "For Humanity's Sake."

Chapter 3

The River, the Rapids

The West Michigan Whitecaps baseball team announced in 2021 that they would partner with Grand Rapids Whitewater, a nonprofit focused on reverting the Grand River to its former glory. The Whitecaps changed their name for one game. The new name, the Grand Rapids Dam Breakers, went along with a new logo, a sturgeon holding a baseball bat. The stunt aimed to raise awareness of the movement to remove the dams from the Grand River and restore the rapids. A *Grand Rapids Press* article noted in 1925 that "this city's original hope to future greatness was based chiefly on the rapids of the Grand."[24]

The Grand River is inseparable from Grand Rapids. The city's name invokes a poetic past, announcing to all that grand, magnificent rapids, torrents of powerful water, once ruled here. Today, walking near the river can evoke this sense: feeling the cool breeze off the water, hearing the water roll past. The river informs so much of the city's past and will play a central role in its future. The city's history abounds with examples of the river as the main character in the story of Grand Rapids, from the days it was a prime mode of transportation to and from the city to its time as a resource of industry. And while many historical accounts detail Grand River stories, there are still stories unexplored.

FORMED ROUGHLY THIRTEEN THOUSAND years ago by glaciers, the Grand River is the longest in the state, flowing through nine cities on its way to Lake Michigan. From the beginning of human history in the area, the river served

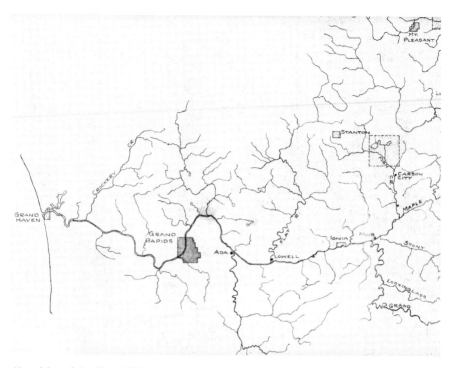

Above: Map of the Grand River waterway. *Grand Rapids City Archives and Records Center.*

Opposite: Map showing the curved wing dam in the Grand River in 1853. *Grand Rapids City Archives and Records Center.*

as a utility. In 2020, the Grand Valley State University Kutsche Office of Local History gathered over twenty organizations involved with local history that spanned the 263-mile waterway. The purpose was to collect stories from the various communities that shared the Grand River. The resulting magazine, *Connections Along the Grand River*, provides excellent details about the river's overall history.

For example, historians Wally and Jane Ewing wrote about the Native American canoe voyages that first made the Grand navigable.[25] These watercrafts became supplemented by the bateaux, flat-bottomed vessels used by the French, and the various skiffs that residents built. Larger steamboats followed. Early settlers made the long journey to the fledgling village, having two main routes available. They would often travel across the land from Detroit to Jackson or Lansing and then take a boat for the remainder of the trip. The other route utilized water highways the whole trip, going from Detroit to Lake Huron, through the Mackinaw Straits down to Grand

Haven, and then up through the Grand River. In 1833, settler Joel Guild noted that supplies often arrived by water from Detroit. River transportation continued to be critical throughout the years. An 1870s ordinance passed by the Common Council forbade ship captains from knowingly bringing sick passengers into the city unless they started showing symptoms aboard the vessel as it traversed the Grand.

In *Connections Along the Grand River*, the Grand Rapids Public Museum wrote about the sturgeon that served as a staple of the Native American diet. Trout and salmon supplemented the sturgeon; all three still swim in the Grand.

While the Native Americans used the Grand River for food and navigation, they did not seek to alter the river to the extent the settlers did. Canals dredged, channels filled in and islands removed: the settlers shaped the river to their needs. The city had to fight the river, though, for the mighty Grand would not go without a fight. The hidden story of the Grand River involves the dams built into the river, battling floods and ice, and the canals.

WRITING TO HIS SISTER in October 1835, Lucius Lyon discussed the canal he was paying to have constructed on the east side of the river. It was sixty to eighty feet wide and five feet deep, and it would let steamers navigate around the rapids and provide a source of power for factories. There were already mills powered by water on the Grand by the time construction began on the canal. Lyon was also paying for a steamboat to traverse the Grand River. In another letter to one of his business partners a few days later, he wrote that fifty men led by an engineer were hard at work on the canal. Digging supplies arrived on a skiff, sent down the river from Jackson.

Lyon sent plans of his canal, drawn by John Almy, to his partners and said that the terminus would need some finagling because it would end near a milldam under Louis Campau's control. The canal was roughly constructed, by no means a feat of precision engineering, and later attempts were made to perfect the waterway. Lyon's leading partner in the canal endeavor was N.O. Sargeant.

The first dam in the city, a type known as a wing dam, rose out of the river in 1849; it directed water into the East Side Canal. Historian Z.Z. Lydens noted that the dam was five feet high and made of stone, gravel, logs and miscellaneous brush. It was built just north of Sixth Street and curved toward Newberry Street. The state legislature gave the supervisors of Kent County permission to construct the dam in conjunction with further work for the East Side Canal. James Davis built the dam, yet the East Side Canal remained unfinished.

Davis was born just outside Niagara Falls in New York, coming to West Michigan when he was six years old in 1836. He must have impressed the city leaders to land the contract for the dam when he was just nineteen years old. Before the days of the city manager mode of governing the city's affairs, Davis acted as a sort of business manager of Grand Rapids. He filled this role by impressing the Board of Public Works with his management skills. His obituary tells the story of how he broke a voting gridlock. Residents had repeatedly voted down bond propositions for an extension of the city sewers, so Davis mapped out which streets had the largest population of voters. The bond proposal added water mains specifically for those streets. The action earned him a spot on the Board of Public Works and his role as the city's de facto business manager.

Three years after Davis built the wing dam, there were efforts to have it removed and rebuilt. The State of Michigan passed an act providing permission to complete the East Side Canal and relocate the wing dam to a lower point in the river. While it may seem odd that the legislature would permit the city to remove the wing dam only three years after it was built, the reason was that the East Side Canal had run into financial trouble. There is no evidence to suggest that the city actually removed the dam around this time. Maps from 1853, 1870, 1873 and 1875 all show the wing dam still standing, as do the 1878 Sanborn maps at the Grand Rapids Public Library. This revelation contradicts a belief in the conventional historical narrative that the wing dam was removed in 1866 when business interests built a waterpower dam.

IN 1865, THE NEWLY formed West Side Water Power Association and the East Side Water Power Company negotiated an agreement to split the rights to use the water from the Grand River. Each agreed to maintain half of a new dam proposed at Fourth Street. According to Albert Baxter, the West Side Water Power Association started construction on the West Side Canal in 1866; they built their portion of the dam to direct water into their canal. The East Side Water Power Company constructed its side of the dam around the same time.

The West Side Canal boasted a much longer lifespan than the East Side Canal. There were calls to close and fill the East Side Canal as early as 1914, and by 1925, city workers had converted the waterworks into a wide sewer. In 1959, city workers began draining the West Side Canal, preparing large amounts of gravel to fill the barren waterway. Eventually, the canal labeled as the most prominent power source for Grand Rapids's industrial arm would become a parking lot. Today, the land has been converted into Ah-Nab-Awen Park and riverfront trails.

The waterpower dam constructed for both canals outlasted both in one form or another. The waterpower dam was roughly 680 feet long and located about 1,450 feet north of Bridge Street Bridge and 800 feet below Sixth Street. At the time it was built, there was no Sixth Street Bridge. Roughly halfway through the dam, a chute was maintained jointly by the two waterpower companies, approximately 22 feet long and used for the logging industry. A report from 1913 by H.N. Byllesby & Company noted that the dam was 10 feet tall and its construction was in the form of what is known as a crib dam. The report stated that the barrier could be raised to 18 feet using flashboards.

The two canals enabled businesses to harness waterpower, empowering industry to flourish and grow. An unseen consequence of the growing business interest in waterpower was the decrease in transportation interests. A *Grand Rapids Press* article in 1925 asserted that businesses petitioned to abandon a lock system in the dams, fearing that if the canals focused on accommodating boats, there would be less water for their factories. The article noted that "in these days river navigation is looked upon as considerable of a joke."[26]

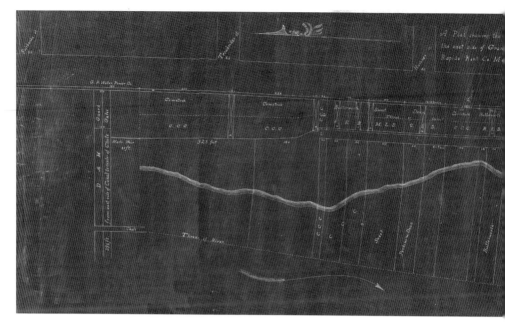

Plat map showing the East Side Canal and east side waterpower dam drawn by Wright L. Coffinberry in 1876. *Grand Rapids City Archives and Records Center.*

THE GRAND RIVER WAS always prone to flooding. The Native Americans anticipated the floods and required their waters to saturate their island crops and remove loose debris. Settlers and the city they built fought against the flooding. It is likely that settlers were also partly at fault for the flooding. Marshes and wetlands happy to soak up annual spring showers were drained and built on, forcing any rain to run right into the river.

The annual spring flooding was also caused in part by what are called ice jams. In a 1907 report, engineer Lyman Cooley, brought to Grand Rapids from Chicago to study the problem of flooding and waterpower development, described the icy situation. He explained how ice could anchor where the water is shallow, where it cannot easily float along the top of the water, causing it to build up and create a natural dam of ice. The piers of bridges often exacerbated the glacial problem by providing buttresses to hold back the ice. A Grand Rapids Historical Commission article noted that in 1838, the ice jammed, and the frozen mass rose twenty to thirty feet high. The city's worst flood happened in 1904, partly caused by an ice jam.

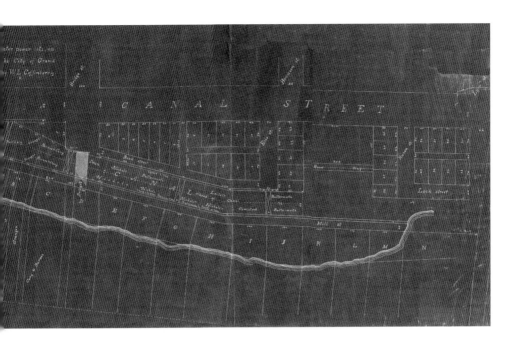

Before the flooding, William T. Powers tried to raise the alarm. Powers, an early settler and prolific industrialist, built the West Side Canal. He went before the City Council and asked the city leaders to take action against the buildup of ice gearing up to spill into the West Side Canal. He said the situation was so bad that if some action was not taken soon, the results "may be very disastrous to the City as well as to ourselves."[27] At the same time, Powers published a short editorial in the *Grand Rapids Press* warning the public that dangerous flooding was imminent.

The flood came and submerged much of the west side of Grand Rapids. Property damage was extensive. This disaster prompted the city to hire consultants and experts to give them a detailed plan of action to prevent another flood. Projects like flood walls and dredging the river to make it deeper marked the first three decades of the twentieth century.

In an attempt to prevent ice from once again adding to the problem, dynamite became the tool of choice. City workers took a small boat onto the river, and once they reached the shelf of ice, they walked to where the jam was, melted a hole in the ice and placed dynamite into the hole. The explosive solution broke the ice, and city workers used long poles to push the ice further down the river. Photographers captured one blast in 1936 as it reached well over thirty feet.

The Grand River filled with ice and snow in 1927 at the Pearl Street Bridge. *Grand Rapids City Archives and Records Center.*

THE FIRST BRIDGES ALLOWED travel across the river without the aid of a canoe for a fee. Tolls and penalties for traveling across the bridges irked both sides of the city. Charles Belknap described one of the early toll bridges as being built of white pine, with latticework on the sides, and covered with pine, noting that a sign warned of a five-dollar fine for riding your horse faster than a walk. Eventually, the bridge was no more, due to a nearby fire that jumped to the flammable pine, forcing some residents over the railing and into the relative safety of the river.

Baxter's *History of Grand Rapids* provides a wealth of detail about the early bridges, documenting their dimensions, materials and uses. Like the bridge Belknap wrote about, those that spanned early Grand Rapids were built of wood, with large stone piers sunk into the riverbed. The first bridge was at Bridge Street, made of wood with eight large stone piers. This crossing was replaced by the one Belknap described. The bridge's piers, thirty-six by eight feet thick at their widest, survived the fire, with subsequent bridges built and rebuilt over their stones. In the 1880s, a wrought-iron bridge replaced the last wooden bridge at Bridge Street, though it still used the original stone piers. This bridge was replaced by a concrete bridge in 1906, which was rebuilt in the 1970s.

City engineering staff using dynamite to break apart ice in the Grand River in 1936. *Grand Rapids City Archives and Records Center.*

The history of the Grand River bridges can be uniquely traced using historical drawings found at the City Archives and Records Center. Intricate drawings, like those of Crescent Park, are shown as artistic masterpieces. Plans for the 1884 Fulton Street Bridge, 1885 Pearl Street Bridge and 1879 Leonard Street Bridge can all be found within the collection. The 1880s Sixth Street Bridge set shows every rivet, every flourish in the intricate design. Shown are not only river bridges but also bridges over the canals and creeks. A small creek that ran through Grandville Avenue near Logan Street worried Emma Field, president of the Kindergarten Association. She asked the Common Council to place a small bridge over the creek so that schoolchildren walking to school just west of Grandville Avenue would not fall into the water. Dams, too, were built outside the river. A dam in the long-gone Creston Park Pond allowed the old settling basin to transition into a favorite watering hole for children to visit.

ANOTHER DAM, LONG GONE, was located at Coldbrook Street, where the Grand Rapids Water Works stood. The dam was built in 1896 for $999, contracted to Charles E. Williams. This dam was hollow timber, 660 feet long and roughly 3 feet tall. The city awarded Williams another contract for $226 a few years later to complete more work on the dam.

This dam garnered immediate opposition. The initial construction ended in November 1896, and by March of the following year, complaints flowed into the Common Council's correspondence. By the beginning of the twentieth century, there was talk of replacing the hollow timber dam with a collapsible barrier. In 1904, there were reports that the waterworks dam was responsible for farms flooding farther up the river. A 1909 *Grand Rapids Herald* article argued that if the city replaced the Fourth Street dam with one of concrete, then it could take down the controversial waterworks dam. Some plans recommended removing the waterworks dam and what was known as the natural rock dam.

The natural rock dam rested at the head of the rapids north of Leonard Street. Lyman Cooley recommended in 1904 and 1907 that the city remove this natural rock dam and that the river be scalped and dredged. The city took this recommendation to heart, and by 1915, the natural rock dam had been removed, at a cost of $250,000.

Around this time, in 1915, the Fourth Street waterpower dam was replaced by concrete. That year, a flood swept down from Lowell, broke the timber crib dam and washed away roughly one hundred feet of the structure. Plans in the Grand Rapids City Archives from 1915 show proposed repairs for ninety feet of dam, one set of plans for timber crib and one for concrete. These were only for the western portion of the dam. Another set of drawings located in the Grand Rapids City Archives, labeled as "Fourth Street dam" and dated 1926, indicate that it was at this time that the remaining Fourth Street dam turned to concrete.

Following the Fourth Street dam, the city concocted a series of concrete "beautification dams." The beautification dams attempted to remedy the harm that had previously bedeviled the river, like the proposals today to remove them. A *Grand Rapids Press* article stated that the years of factories using the river left the waterway "a rocky, weedy, rubbish-strewn waste—a disappointment to visitors, a source of humiliation to residents."[28]

A series of five dams would make the river more visually appealing. In March 1926, the City Commission noted that it had finalized plans for the first two beautification dams. The first was one hundred feet north of the Bridge Street Bridge, and the second was built just below the bridge.

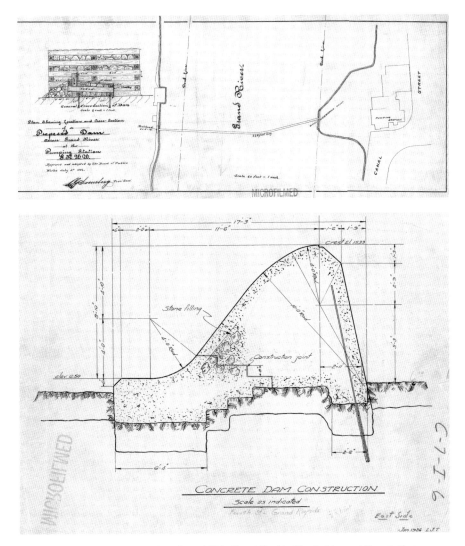

Top: Plan of the waterworks dam from 1896. *Grand Rapids City Archives and Records Center*.

Bottom: Engineering drawing of the concrete dam to replace the east side of the Fourth Street dam in 1926. *Grand Rapids City Archives and Records Center*.

The third was north of the Gillet Bridge, and the fourth was north of the Pearl Street Bridge. These were all erected in the summer of 1927. The set of plans showed the fifth dam just below the Fulton Street Bridge, but it seems that it was either not constructed or so low as to be unnoticeable.

Concrete beautification dam in a drained Grand River just north of the Bridge Street Bridge in 1927. *Grand Rapids City Archives and Records Center.*

THERE IS NO DOUBT that the Grand River has seen abuse since the settling of the Grand River Valley. This fact has echoed time and time again. The *Grand Rapids Press* noted in 1970 that "visiting urban planners have been simultaneously enthralled by the possibilities the river offers, both aesthetically and practically, and appalled by the neglect it has received."[29] The current dichotomy is the river's potential for innovative placemaking and the acknowledgment of our forebears' sins in harming the river. In the city's early days, there seemed to be an acknowledgment of this as well.

In 1851, Louis Campau proposed a resolution to the Common Council to prohibit mills and factories from dumping garbage into the Grand River. They were using the East Side Canal for waterpower and would dump their industrial byproducts right into the water. The Common Council also passed an ordinance prohibiting individuals from using the Grand River as a bathtub, but only in the daytime. The resolution was in the interest of public health, not necessarily for the health of the Grand River.

Historian Kayne Ferrier has extensively and comprehensively researched the city's sewage treatment history. Ferrier wrote that sewage would initially drain into ditches or pipes leading directly into the river. On the west side, the notorious and noxious Big Ditch was one such ditch constructed in 1874. Ferrier also noted that residents would dump garbage and waste into the natural creeks such as Coldbrook on the east side. The State of Michigan eventually demanded that Grand Rapids cease dumping sewage directly into the river. In the 1930s, the Sewage Treatment Plant helped keep the river from receiving further raw sewage.

OVER THE YEARS, BRIDGES have been rebuilt; sunken art installations have come and gone; walls have replaced the natural edges of the river, and eventually, slowly, the river has been beautified. Trails were added along the river, continuing a tradition of making the river the city's pride once more. Far more history lies sunken in the depths of the river. Homer L. Burch, a local historian and Grand River researcher, spent much of his later years uncovering the river's secrets. In a *Grand Rapids Press* article, he stated that a comprehensive, conclusive work on the Grand River would take forty years or more to complete. Clearly, there is more to uncover in the Grand River.

CHAPTER 4

BOULDERS AND BRICKS,
STEEL AND GLASS

Before factories and commercial buildings lined either side of Leonard Street NW on the shore of the Grand, the area was a neighborhood long before US 131 ran parallel to the river. A city market sat on the northeast corner of Front Avenue and Leonard, serving the houses that ran up and down Front Avenue whose backyards butted up against the river's edge.

In 1913, a sign went up in the neighborhood, on the lawn of 1252 Front Avenue NW, just a few lots north of Leonard Street. The sign read, "This Rock Free." The house's resident, William Timmer, knew that all who saw the sign would understand what it referred to. Behind the homes, along the edge of the river, a mountain of limestone rubble loomed over houses. The stone, described by the press as weighing one million tons, was a product of dredging and scalping the river.

Experts recommended dredging the river in response to the 1904 flood that put much of Leonard Street underwater. The city contracted with G.W. Bunker and Co., owned by George Bunker, to build a series of flood walls and excavate the river. City leaders also contemplated employing Bunker to dispose of the stone at thirty-seven cents per cubic yard of rubble. However, the aldermen concluded that the bid was too expensive and unnecessary, despite calls from citizens that the pile of rocks was a nuisance.

Stone quarried from the river was sought after as solid building material in the city's early years. The city hoped it could find a use or a buyer for the stone. Stone schoolhouses, homes and public buildings constructed from

Dredge working on the Grand River at Leonard Street. *Grand Rapids City Archives and Records Center.*

riverbed stones were scattered through Grand Rapids. The exterior of St. Mark's Episcopal Church, the oldest public building in Grand Rapids, was built in the late 1840s from stone hauled out of the river by teams of oxen. Surveyor John Almy built the first stone house in the city in 1839. River rubble also became wall filler for many buildings.

The stone taken from the river at the beginning of the twentieth century was deemed unfit as a building material. This change marked a turning point in building practices. From the 1890s to just after the beginning of the twentieth century, construction in the city experienced a drastic change. Building trends influenced not only how the city looked aesthetically but also its very fabric. Winston Churchill once proclaimed, "We shape our buildings; thereafter they shape us."

While the soul of Grand Rapids is its people, its body forms out of the physical. Wood, stone, brick, concrete, steel and glass rise from the earth and dive into it. Homes and businesses, streets, curbs, sidewalks, sewers and pipes all join to compose the city's infrastructure.

Carl Sandburg, the poet and historian well known for his descriptions of Chicago, once mused, "I have often wondered what it is an old building can do to you when you happen to know a little about things that went on long ago."[30] The trends in constructing the city's infrastructure can also provide a deeper understanding of and appreciation for the place. Understanding the literal building blocks of the city can shed light on why the city looks and feels the way it does.

The early structures in the city were little more than log cabins. These were supplemented and eventually replaced by frame buildings. Plaster walls, stone foundations and slate roofs all became standard. Brick also became standard.

Grand Rapids has many handsome facades made of brick, and sidewalks and streets of brick disperse throughout the city. From ancient Egypt to modern Michigan, bricks have adorned buildings. Several brickmakers left their mark on the city, monuments that still stand today.

John Davis was the first brickmaker in the early days, having set up a few kilns in 1834 at a clay deposit he discovered near the corner of Oakes and South Division. Davis only operated his kilns for one or two years, ostensibly moving on to bigger and better things. The *Grand Rapids Press* noted that in the early days, brick was made by hand, shaped into molds and then wheeled to large kilns.

Solomon Withey was the next brick entrepreneur in the city. He opened a brick-firing kiln near the corner of Coldbrook and Ionia, but the brick was of poor quality, and the first structure he made, a chimney, collapsed. His son Orison had better luck. The younger Withey dug into a clay deposit near Division and Oakes, where Davis had first bored, and it was from his store that many early brick buildings could claim origin.

Baxter's *History of Grand Rapids* is filled with instances of early brick buildings being constructed by well-known Grand Rapids names. The first substantial brick building was Irving Hall, built by Samuel Ball in 1843. Brick allowed the buildings to rise into the sky higher than before. Irving Hall rose three stories, towering at that time on Monroe Center near Pearl.

The first half of the 1850s saw a fair amount of brick buildings. The first four-story building, made of brick in 1855, was called Colins Hall. Large iron columns aided the height of the building on the ground floors. Much of the brick was most likely imported. Orison's kilns could not keep up with demand. Baxter noted that in 1854, roughly eighty thousand bricks were imported. He also stated that in 1873, contractors used as many as twenty million bricks. Specialty brick was also imported; cream-colored bricks came from Milwaukee. It was Simeon L. Baldwin who became the most prominent brickmaker and filled some of this need.

Piles of bricks to be used for sidewalk construction on Lyon Street in 1935. *Grand Rapids City Archives and Records Center.*

An early pioneer who immigrated to the city in 1844, Baldwin built his brickmaking company with his partner and brother-in-law David Seymour, until Seymour died in 1863. Their output of bricks started at three hundred thousand a year and grew to highs of six million a year.

Baldwin served as an alderman for many years before being elected to the state legislature. He opened his brickyard operation in 1885 near the corner of Fountain and Fuller, which was the eastern edge of the city at that time. Baldwin eventually sold his operation to Brown, Clark & Co. Eventually, the majority of brick manufacturers were combined into the Grand Rapids Consolidated Brick and Tile Company, operating an extensive collection of kilns and clay pits near Baldwin's old operation. The neighborhood became known as the brickyard, and historic signs bearing the name still adorn buildings around the area, with the Dutch "Brikyaat" displayed.

BRICK WAS NOT ONLY built toward the heavens but also sunk into the ground. Water basins, pipes and brick sewers ran like roots throughout the earth. Individual brick or stone wells were common in the village's early days. Brick sewers eventually replaced open ditches and creek culverts. Monroe Center boasted the first brick sewer, built in 1856.

While the city ran the sewers, consumer water flowed through a private company, the Grand Rapids Hydraulic Company. When contractors turned over the earth for the sewer in Monroe, the Hydraulic Company laid its first iron pipe. Once dirt buried the pipes, cobblestones paved the street.

In 1875, after an extensive section on the city's northeast side burned down, the city decided it would need to provide an alternative water source. The common council selected a swath of land where the Coldbrook Creek and the Carrier Creek met on the recommendation of an engineer the Common Council had hired from Albany. The ground naturally dipped, and the city built a basin to hold the water. They used bricks to line the bottom of the basin and cobblestone to line the walls.

Carrier and Coldbrook Creek Sewer, showing brick and concrete pipes. *Grand Rapids City Archives and Records Center.*

A dam was built across Carrier Creek to create a large pond over the basin. The settling basin was used for only about five years, becoming obsolete when a new reservoir adorned Belknap Hill. The city abandoned the settling basin in part due to the poor water quality of the creeks. One record shows that local pigs occasionally bathed in the streams that flowed into the pond.

In 1900, the basin was abandoned and became a nuisance. The press called it a menace to public health. Thieves had started to pilfer the bricks and cobblestones from the basin, prompting the Board of Public Works to post a ten-dollar reward for any arrest made of those carrying away the materials. The city tried selling the materials, like it would try to do for the river stone.

Eventually, the course of action with the least resistance was overflowing the basin with water and turning the area into a park. The park and subsequent pond became a favorite swimming hole for local children. Later, the park became the site of a housing development.

While brick is still employed heavily today, its importance diminished when concrete became the dominant building material.

In 1890, THE VALLEY City and Oak Hill Cemeteries built a new office building. Nineteen years later, the Grand Rapids Parks and Recreation Department constructed the first pavilion in John Ball Park. The building specifications for both structures, now stored within the Grand Rapids City Archives, provide an insightful look into how construction methods drastically changed during that time.

Builders used concrete in both projects. The Oak Hill specifications noted that the crushed stone to be mixed should be "not larger than hen's eggs."[31] The John Ball Park specifications used no such folksy measurement guidelines.

The Oak Hill building was wood framed. Wood floor joists rested on wooden girders, which sat on brick piers. Iron and steel were reserved for roof moldings and the cornices. The roof itself was of slate.

For the John Ball Park pavilion, steel replaced wood girders. Columns of steel supported the building. Open-hearth steel reinforced any poured concrete. The specifications noted that builders should adhere to the new manufacturing standards for utilizing steel. Beams and lintels were of metal, and floors were reinforced with metal.

At the turn of the century, steel was becoming more prominent. The first steel skyscraper rose in Chicago in 1885; Grand Rapids began toying with the idea of working with steel. In 1898, city leaders discussed building a

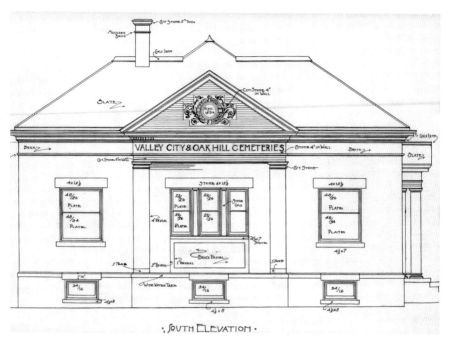

Oak Hill Cemetery office building blueprint. *Grand Rapids City Archives and Records Center.*

new public library out of "steel and stone."[32] One of the first buildings that utilized steel was the Grand Rapids Brewing Company on Michigan Avenue.

From the 1890s to 1920, some of the most iconic Grand Rapids buildings ascended into the cityscape. Those that are still around were those built, in part, with steel. In 1892, the Michigan Trust Building was constructed. The higher floors of the McKay tower climbed in 1915. In 1913, the Pantlind was built.

With the new construction methods came risks. As buildings grew taller, steelworkers ran a higher risk of falling. Twenty-nine-year-old John Kepple fell from the steel skeleton of the Herpolsheimer's new addition. He experienced a bout of vertigo and fell from the steel beam onto the roof of the adjacent building, breaking both his legs. The riveter had been working above the ninth story. Kepple survived, though he never fully recovered. His accident was the first during the building of Herpolsheimer's.

Safety became one of the city's most significant concerns during this time, not only for construction reasons but also due to fire safety. When the Clarendon Hotel suffered from a disastrous fire in 1903, the papers argued it was time for stricter building regulations.

Because of these developments and the fast growth, the city began looking into implementing a building ordinance and having a building inspector. The first attempts at creating an updated building ordinance and having an official building inspector met with controversy. In 1893, the city had three building inspectors, but the position did not come with pay, and the rumor mills insisted they did not do much inspection work.

In 1892, the city had a group of builders, architects and city leaders draft a building ordinance. The ordinance died in committee, and two years later, the Common Council delegated three inspectors to write the new building ordinance. In January 1894, the inspectors submitted their ten-page ordinance and a bill for $312.50 for the work. The regulations within did not incite much controversy. The bill, however, outraged the Common Council and the city at large. An anonymous city official stated in the press, "They know and I know that $312 worth of time was never put in by those men on framing that ordinance."[33]

Indeed, much of the ordinance seemed copied from the ordinance proposed two years prior. However, the city reluctantly paid the bill, and the regulations became city law. The building inspector was under the jurisdiction of the Board of Fire and Police Commissioners, appointed by

John Ball Park pavilion circa 1927. *Grand Rapids City Archives and Records Center.*

Scrip laborers working on streets and homes in 1932. *Grand Rapids City Archives and Records Center.*

the Common Council. Any individual, group or company hoping to build in the city first had to apply to the inspector for a permit. Something akin to that practice is still required today.

The inspectors also worked with engineers to inspect building materials for public works projects. In 1904, an engineer condemned upward of seven thousand bricks during a city project to pave Ellsworth Avenue.

The early decades of the twentieth century saw the formation of more strategic city planning. The Grand Rapids Planning Commission arose in 1919, with Charles W. Garfield as a founding member. The Planning Department started in earnest in May 1921, and a zoning ordinance was enacted in 1922, splitting the city into five districts.

Building heights and types were relegated to different parts of the city. Citizens could, of course, petition for a variance. The Board of Zoning Appeals was appointed, and the first variance was brought to them in 1923 for re-platting two lots on Calvin Avenue to comply with the residential district.

ANOTHER TREND THAT EMERGED during the construction upheaval was that of glass bending. In the late 1890s, bent glass became popular for storefronts and even for some residential buildings. In 1900, only four or five glass-bending factories operated in the whole of the United States, and two were in Grand Rapids.

The Furniture City Glass Bending Works operated out of the Widdicomb complex on the northwest side of town. The factory had several large kilns it used to heat glass. Workers would judge the kiln's heat by the color of the flames. Glass can bend at 1,800 degrees Fahrenheit, but it would melt at 2,300 degrees. Once the kiln reached the correct temperature, workers would fix glass into molds mounted on cars so workers could wheel them in and out of the enormous kilns.

The Furniture City Glass Bending Works was the first glass-bending company in the city. The second was the short-lived Grand Rapids Glass Bending Company. The second, more notorious, company opened a factory on the northeast corner of Bond and Newberry. The company operated for only ten months before going bankrupt. Unfortunately, when the press published a story about the bankruptcy, it named the wrong company, and customers and workers of the Furniture City Glass Bending Works were shocked to read that their company was bankrupt—when in reality, it was the other glass company.

Today, when viewing the Grand Rapids cityscape, buildings of glass glitter in the sun. The Bridgewater Place, the Amway Grand Plaza and the JW Marriott all reach toward the heavens, the sun reflected on their faces.

POSSIBLY NO OTHER CONSTRUCTION project altered the face of Grand Rapids more than that of the urban renewal and the building of US 131 and I-196. Much has been written and explored about that era of change. Little, however, has been studied about the subsequent program known as Model Cities.

The Model Cities program, conceived under President Lyndon B. Johnson, was a part of his Great Society program. The Model Cities program focused on creating new housing and community resources by relying on citizen participation. Grand Rapids was chosen along with 150 other municipalities to participate. A new city department, the City Demonstration Agency (CDA) formed to manage the new projects specifically. It received advice and recommendations from a Model Cities Committee composed of members of the target area.

US 131 construction using steel beams. *Grand Rapids City Archives and Records Center.*

The target area was designated Wealthy Street south toward Hall Street and Union west toward Godfrey, considered the inner city. The location was predominantly African American and Latino, due in part to housing discrimination practices in other parts of the city. Overcrowding was one of the main concerns of the Model Cities program, as were the poor housing conditions those residents faced.

In 1968, a group of community members, almost all of whom had past connections with the NAACP housing committee, joined to form a nonprofit called Freedom Homes. The nonprofit's goal was to provide low-income housing through what they dubbed "sweat equity." They wanted the community to have a hand in building the homes in their neighborhood.

The nonprofit was awarded a contract from the City Demonstration Agency to construct several single-family homes, rehabilitate run-down properties for resale and provide jobs for residents in the target area.

Freedom Homes built its first house in 1968 at 719 Prospect Avenue SE. Still there to this day, the building is a modest one-story home. The papers noted that this was the first new home built in the inner city in fifty years.

Jerome Sorrells was the first president of Freedom Homes and received a commendation from Governor George Romney. Sorrells noted that "while the financing is from the white community, the organization, decision-making and construction are controlled by the black community."[34] Despite the early positive press, the organization soon received much scrutiny and criticism.

Part of this stemmed from an attempt from outside organizations, whose members did not live within the Model Cities target neighborhood, to wrest control of the inner-city housing away from Freedom Homes. The Community Action Program group, the federal branch of the anti-poverty program, claimed that Freedom Homes was mismanaged and chaotic and sought to supplant the nonprofit as the head of low-income housing developments in the inner city.

The levied claim of mismanagement followed Freedom Homes throughout its organizational life. Article after article claims that the nonprofit built only one or two properties. The year before he became president, Gerald R. Ford even asked the Government Accountability Office to investigate the Model Cities program and Freedom Homes to determine if malfeasance was present. They found no evidence of wrongdoing but again leveled the accusation that the program had accomplished very little and built only two houses.

The records kept by the City Demonstration Agency, now a defunct department, paint a different picture. The records show that Freedom Homes built at least fourteen houses in an area that desperately needed more housing, utilizing "sweat equity" so that Black community members aided in the construction.

719 Prospect Ave SE, the first home built by Freedom Homes. *Grand Rapids City Archives and Records Center.*

Jesse Thomas, a father of eight, helped build 617 Sheldon Avenue SE. A residence at 525 Crawford Street SE was built with the help of local high school seniors. A house on 1229 Euclid was built with the help of the family who purchased it.

The project was maligned severely, despite apparent successes. It ended in 1974 when funding for the Model Cities program ended. The need for housing did not cease, though. As the city was looking at new modes of housing, alternatives arose. Condominiums were first built in Grand Rapids in the 1970s. Grand Rapids sought other innovative solutions: factory-built buildings, demolition bans, homesteading and a "paint and fix by 1976" plan. One success story arose from the multitude, the ICCF. The Inner-City Christian Federation started in 1974, the year Freedom Homes closed.

GRAND RAPIDS IS A city built of wood, stone, steel, cement, glass and many other materials. The construction materials informed how the city was structured, the buildings' heights and the city's industry. The changes in construction birthed a movement of inspection and oversight that is still around today. Construction projects with lasting impact are myriad, from the dredging of the river to the construction of low-income housing. The built city informs all.

CHAPTER 5

FUR AND FEATHERS

Wright Lewis Coffinberry was woken up far before dawn on May 2, 1855, by a banging on his wall. When he went to investigate, he found that his neighbor's cow had wandered over to his lot and begun eating the grass next to his home, knocking its head against the wall to reach the blades.

Coffinberry was none too pleased and took his neighbor, John Hart, to court to seek damages. After settling the matter at the courthouse just before the case began, Coffinberry made his neighbor promise to keep his cow better guarded and promised to drop the suit.

Coffinberry's short diary entry about the incident shows how prevalent animals were in the city's early days. Wild animals such as bears, wolves and wildcats appear in narratives of the pioneer era.

Even in modern times, when the wilderness has turned into concrete and skyscrapers, animals still are a large part of the city. Dog parks are scattered throughout the city, cats lounge in some store windows and sparrows can be found eating crumbs outside coffee shops. The stories full of fur and feathers are not often those told in local history circles, but they offer a fascinating glimpse into our more animalistic history.

NATIVE AMERICANS HAD DOMESTICATED dogs before the incursion of white settlers. The canine companions functioned as pets and partners in hunting and guarding settlements.

Grand Rapids Parks and Rec employee working at a dog training class held in one of the parks. *Grand Rapids City Archives and Records Center.*

When settlers arrived in the Grand River Valley, dogs traveled with them. Baxter notes that when the settlers arrived in their wagons, "dogs walked beside them."[35] Dogs also served a more practical purpose to those villagers. In 1837, the first paper established in the village, the *Grand River Times*, was written with supplies brought to the city by dogsleds on the frozen Grand River, trekking from Grand Haven. Baxter also noted that in 1858, a dog helped three hunters take down bears when they encroached too far into the city. In "Yesterdays of Grand Rapids," Charles Belknap mentioned he would take his canoe out into the river with his dog for some quality time.

Bears, along with wolves and wildcats, were present and a problem. Baxter noted that bears and wolves would wander into the city occasionally. Many city residents raised pigs and cows, and the wild animals would prey on the animals residents kept in small pens in their yards. The Village Board of Trustees authorized a bounty on wolves, offering $5 for every wolf, worth $140 today.

THE WILD PREDATORS WERE especially a problem for one of the most influential animals in the city: horses. Sources on how many individuals kept horses are sparse. Baxter discusses horses mainly concerning specific owners, noting if a horse was shot or how many horses it took to complete a task. He also discussed the many livery barns and stables where horses boarded.

The first known livery was built in 1847 and stood roughly where Louis Campau Promenade is now. It had only a few horses that residents could rent. This operation became one of the most preeminent early liveries and was known as the Omnibus Stable. Next to the barn sat the Eagle Hotel, the first hotel in the city. Horses and carriages were readily available to rent for hotel patrons and anyone else in town in need of a steed.

City Wholesale Market showing the horse-drawn wagons filled with goods for sale in 1911. *Grand Rapids City Archives and Records Center.*

The liveries around town formed a group called the Grand Rapids Hack Owners' Association. The word *hack*, rarely used today, described a horse for hire; its etymology dates back to Hackney, Middlesex, a county in England known for raising fine horses.

Horses were the primary mode of transportation around town, aside from one's own two legs. Numerous liveries were established and highly patronized. The city often hired horses from liveries for departmental use. When the Common Council first proposed the Building Ordinance, it contained a section stating that a horse and buggy would be available to the building inspector. Coffinberry would rent a horse and carriage when his surveys required. Liveries competed like companies do today. In 1899, the Grand Rapids liveries ran deals for carriages that were rented for funerals. They cost two dollars instead of the usual three.

By 1894, the most extensive livery was operated by James P. Moran. Moran immigrated to Kent County from Ireland as a young boy. His lifelong love of horses began when he worked as a farmhand in Walker. He opened a small livery soon after in Grand Rapids. He was known as an expert horse rider, and many of his livery horses gathered acclaim from competitions. He built his stable on Division Avenue, where the Keeler building now sits. A *Grand Rapids Herald* article provided excellent details about the stable. Carriages and other vehicles resided on the first floor, along with the tack, saddles and offices. The horses lived on the second floor, with fifty individual stalls sporting lofts overhead for feed. The building even boasted a basement for extra vehicles.

Hotels and other businesses kept small liveries for patrons and visitors. Many individuals had stables in lieu of garages. Neighborhoods depicted in the 1878 Sanborn fire insurance maps preserved by the Grand Rapids Public Library show a few residential stables. However, the 1894 maps showed significantly more residents had stables, likely keeping horses or other animals in them. Reviewing the Sanborn maps gives an excellent insight into the growth of stables within the city. Ottawa Avenue from Newberry Street to Mason had one stable in 1878, and by 1895, it had five. This trend followed the growth of the community and the need for residents to travel somewhat farther for work.

Businesses also relied heavily on horses. Companies delivered goods with horses, bringing their wares to market in horse-drawn wagons. The city departments maintained a fleet of steeds, depending on the horses for both fire and police wagons. The Grand Rapids Historical Commission noted that in 1897, the Fire Department had fifty-three horses employed. Public

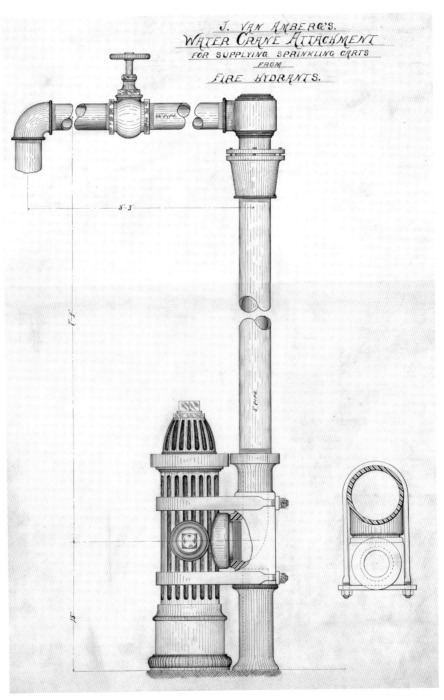

Plan for a water crane attachment for supplying horse-drawn watering carts. *Grand Rapids City Archives and Records Center.*

works also employed several horses. A horse-drawn wagon would be filled to the brim with leaves during fall and with snow during winter. Garbage wagons were pulled by horses as well. Some fire hydrants were designed with a large pipe jutting above to allow horse-drawn watering carts to pull underneath and get water.

Eventually, however, the horse was overtaken by the automobile. In 1923, when cars seemed to have mostly replaced the horse among central city residents, the public works department still had seventeen horses for their work, but they had purchased three cars for their fleet. One year later, their cavalry dropped to nine horses and three in 1925. By 1926, horses had been phased out of use by the department.

The *Grand Rapids Herald* published an article in 1914, republished in the Grand Rapids Historical Society's newsletter, mentioning a firefighter's attitudes toward the addition of a six-cylinder car, replacing his familiar horses: "I'll tell you, it's almost like losing a brother."

Horses were not just beasts of burden. Horse racing became a popular pastime, often to the chagrin of some residents. In 1862, the Common Council passed a resolution that authorized the marshal to punish horse racers and riders and carriage drivers who drove "immoderately." In 1869,

City Lighting Plant staff with their fleet of vehicles in line with the horses employed circa 1924. *Grand Rapids City Archives and Records Center.*

the Grand Rapids Horse Association was formed and became famed for putting on races and holding contests at the local fairs. The first Grand Rapids Horse Association race delighted spectators in 1870.

The Common Council also tried to deal with horses running wild and loose horses. In 1860, they levied a fine of five dollars on an owner whose horse damaged a tree within the city. The poundmaster was also authorized to round up any horses found running loose. Multiple departments filed claims to the Common Council for reimbursement for injuries caused by and to horses.

Horses were sometimes used as payment. One example found within the Common Council proceedings was in 1865. A Mr. Berkley entered into a contract with the city that stipulated he be paid two horses for his work.

While the horse population has decreased in the city, there are still ways to interact with these equine animals. Residents can book horse carriage rides downtown and view *The American Horse*, the twenty-four-foot-tall bronze equine sculpture at the Frederik Meijer Gardens and Sculpture Park.

Canines have long lived in the city, but despite being integral to the Native American settlements and the early settlers, they seemed to receive some animosity when the city adopted its charter. One of the early taxes on residents was for dogs. The city created a special ordinance on dogs, likely due to a petition ninety-two citizens submitted to the Common Council asking for the "suppression" of dogs in the city. The ordinance's language betrayed some early residents' attitudes toward canines. The rule stated, "Every person residing in this city owning or having in his possession, or suffering to be kept on his or her premises, any dog…" That the Common Council used the wording "suffering to be kept" to describe dog ownership seems like a harsh indictment.

The ordinance updated the license fees for dogs, as well. For the first dog, an owner would pay fifty cents per year. The owner would pay another two dollars per year for every additional dog. The ordinance also stipulated that only male or neutered female dogs could be pets. Most likely, this was an attempt to keep the stray dog population down.

Stray dogs were aplenty, and there were not yet any services that cared for wayward canines. As cruel as it sounds, it was not illegal for a resident to shoot a dog thought to be a stray. The marshal was required to watch for any dogs they believed to be strays. They even required owners to pay a ten-dollar fee if their dog seemed to have a "ferocious character or

No. 3   **MALE DOG LICENSE**   **$1.25**
Expires May 1, 1917

NOT GOOD UNTIL

City of Grand Rapids, Michigan

4/6 191 6

STAMPED PAID

To Whom it May Concern:

In consideration of the sum of One Dollar and Twenty-five Cents, paid to the City Treasurer, whose receipt must be hereon affixed, the City of Grand Rapids hereby grants LICENSE to
A. M. Phillips residing at 415 Dudley Ave. N. E.
to keep a Male Dog, described as follows: Airdale & Cocker Spaniel
answering to the name of Nig
according to an ordinance, entitled "An Ordinance Relating to Dogs," passed and approved April 23, 1906.

NOT TRANSFERABLE, except that if dog is sold, the License goes with the sale, but should be reported to City Clerk, so that proper record can be made. This License not valid until presented to the City Treasurer and the amount indicated paid him and his receipt therefor endorsed hereon.

James Schriver City Clerk.

This page, top: Grand Rapids male dog license from 1916. *Grand Rapids City Archives and Records Center.*

This page, bottom: Grand Rapids Parks and Recreation Department hosting a dogsled competition in 1961. *Grand Rapids City Archives and Records Center.*

Opposite: Barney, the first dog to join the Grand Rapids Police Department. *Grand Rapids City Archives and Records Center.*

disposition." The welfare department, too, was required to deny aid to anyone who owned a dog.

Dogs were indeed kept as pets, though. Every spring, residents would apply to the Assessor's Department and later the City Clerk's Office for a dog license. One resident donated a license to the Grand Rapids City Archives and Records Center. In 1917, the cocker spaniel lived on Dudley Avenue NE. City departments would also supply dog license tags. One such dog license tag survives in the Grand Rapids Public Museum. It is from 1897, made from copper, engraved with "GD Rapids Dog Tax/1897/Female/67." The Parks Department also held dog-training sessions for a number of years.

Dogs were also entertainment. In 1886, a dog race took place on Jefferson Avenue between several greyhounds, two of which were named Clothesline and Frankfort. One hundred dollars went to the dog—or his owner—who won. Clothesline ended up the winner. Dogsledding races also took place during the winter. The Grand Rapids Parks Department hosted dogsledding at Richmond Park.

In 1968, A SEVENTEEN-YEAR-OLD attempted to break into the Mt. Vernon Bar on a warm summer morning before dawn. Police officer Robert Eakley happened to be patrolling nearby and startled the youth. The kid ran to a nearby junkyard on Winter Avenue and soon disappeared among the mountains of rusted-out cars. Soon, a furry rookie of the police force, the German Shepherd Barney, was on the trail.

The police dog joined the force in September 1966, owned and trained by Sergeant Donald Worpel. The *Grand Rapids Press* noted that Worpel had paid for all Barney's police training. He must have had an affinity for German Shepherds, because the press also noted he had seven of the loyal hounds.

Once Barney joined the force, working exclusively with Worpel, he soon earned his badge. In May 1968, Barney and Worpel were honored after tracking a group of men who had held up and robbed a bank on State Street SE. Once Barney entered the junkyard to search for the young burglar, it took the canine no time at all to uncover the youth among some bushes. He clearly had the nose for crime solving. In November, Barney, the fur-covered crime fighter, was promoted to sergeant.

Due to the problem of strays, the city created the pound, empowering a poundmaster to round up wandering dogs. The poundmaster was also to take control of other animals that seemed to be ownerless. The pound, established in 1839, was run by the poundmaster, John W. Pierce. Pierce came to Grand Rapids in 1836 and was a prominent member of society. Oddly, while he was the poundmaster, he also operated one of Grand Rapids's early bookstores, built its early concert halls and owned several other business ventures. While he served as poundmaster for only a few years, he also served simultaneously as the village clerk, the township clerk and the secretary of the Grand Rapids Lyceum, the precursor to the Grand Rapids Public Museum. A man named Philander Tracy assumed the role of poundmaster when Pierce stepped down.

Pigs often found themselves residents of the pound. Homeowners would raise pigs in pens on their property for food, and cities would employ pigs to break down garbage. However, like horses and dogs, the swine would break free and roam wild. In the 1850s, the city leaders adopted a swine ordinance that stipulated the number of pigs residents could raise and laid out boundaries for where the pigs could and could not roam free. If the marshal or poundmaster came across a pig, it became a resident of the pound.

Since swine were a source of food, a source of livelihood, the pound often treated them differently than it did dogs. Owners would travel to the pound to retrieve their lost hogs, paying fifty cents per twenty-four hours of custody for every swine. If the pigs stayed in the pound for more than three days, the poundmaster could do with them what he wanted. This privilege often meant selling pigs at auction after placing a mandatory forty-eight-hour notice of the time and place of the auction. Stray dogs held for too long suffered a far worse fate. The city used a garbage incinerator operated by the Public Works Department to rid itself of unneeded animals. The conditions of the pound were terrible. However, sentiment toward animals started improving.

In 1883, the Humane Society of Kent County, originally called the Society for the Prevention of Cruelty to Animals, was organized. The Humane Society employed agents, who were made deputy sheriffs and had the jurisdiction and power to arrest in cases of "cruelty by willful injury, or neglect, or sport."[36]

The *Grand Rapids Herald* noted the activities of the agents relating to horses in a January 1894 article. Agents ordered eight horses to be blanketed from the cold; three reprimands were given for injuring or neglecting horses. In

March of that year, humane agents worked with union teamsters to reduce the height of wagon sides so that the horses would not need to pull as heavy a load. Horses seemed to be the most documented in the paper as having received aid. This focus on horses may be because they were more visible to humane agents or possibly due to their utilitarian use. The Humane Society assisted neglected or abused children as well.

Humane Society agents kept busy protecting the safety of animals. One press article stated that Humane Society agent Eugene Randolph arrested a man for starving two horses and feeding another horse to chickens. Agents blamed the Public Works Department for improperly paving Monroe Center when eight horses broke their legs slipping on the cobblestones.

Sometimes, the humane agents worked with the poundmasters, providing information on loose animals and their monthly activities. This relationship changed when abuses by the poundmasters began to surface. In 1899, the police arrested the poundmaster on the recommendation of the Humane Society. The poundmaster had put a rope around a loose dog's neck and begun to drag it down the road. Bystanders tried to stop him, and when that failed, they tried to loosen the rope from the dog's throat, only to be met with a revolver drawn by the poundmaster. The men backed away from the armed poundmaster and let him continue to drag the dog. He only made it a few yards down the street before the dog expired due to suffocation. This event seems to have started the pound and the Humane Society down a path of animus.

The clash between the Humane Society and the pound culminated when the *Herald* discovered the condition of the animals. On July 15, 1904, the headline read, "Dog Pound Is a Disgrace to City." The reporter described the building as "small, unpainted, ill smelling, filthy…sides full of holes, gnawed by imprisoned canines…emitting a stench sufficient to overcome the odors that permeate the vicinity."[37] The pound was in the southwestern portion of the city, near where the wastewater treatment plant is now and conspicuously near a glue factory and the Pere Marquette Roundhouse.

The reporter noted that the cacophony of noise was overpowering and could easily be heard up to half a mile away. Physical abuse enforced submission. Obscene details of the conditions were described, detailing the helpless animals' miserable plight.

Once the article was published, the police and fire commissioners vowed to act. A clipping published the next day described how the poor conditions caused hundreds of residents to object to the treatment. Humane agent Randolph promised to make a full investigation of the pound. Despite the horrid conditions and a promise to act, the Police and Fire Commission would do nothing to remedy the plight of the dogs. The *Herald* noted that it "looks like the whole matter is now up to Humane Agent Randolph."[38]

Part of the problem, it seemed, was that a new pound had been in the works for some time. Months before the *Herald* article was published, the Common Council debated where to build the new pound. However, every ward strongly opposed the pound residing in their jurisdiction. The pound was outside the city's main stretch, but some council members wanted it placed on the island in the Grand River: out of sight, out of mind. The negotiations had stalled, which may have added to the poor conditions of their current facility.

The *Herald* continued to build momentum by publishing the dire conditions of the dogs. Agent Randolph inspected the pound, bringing along a reporter, a man named Samuel W. Glover. Randolph tried to pressure pound workers to testify and get hard evidence to make an arrest but seemed unable to. It did not help that feelings toward dogs had not changed for everyone in the city. The *Grand Rapids Press* wrote, "It is true there are scores of unlicensed dogs in the city, and many of them are absolutely worthless,"[39] only fractionally redeeming itself by saying the dogs themselves were not at fault.

Once Randolph and Glover accrued enough evidence, Randolph worked with a prosecuting attorney to arrest the master of the pound, Patrick Malone, for cruelty. Malone went before the police court in 1904 but was found not guilty. The case hinged on a specific incident where Malone beat a small dog over the head with a club. The witnesses could not say whether or not the dog had died, so the jury returned with an unfavorable verdict. It did not help that the *Grand Rapids Press* seemed to malign the case, and the judge was also the lawyer for Malone.

The City Commission ended up relenting and moved to build a new pound on the island, next to the garbage burner, much to the chagrin of the First Ward. The new pound seemed to have more adequate facilities and was better suited for the dogs' needs while they waited to be picked up by owners or adopted. The Humane Society of Kent County had been instrumental in achieving this win for the canines. Not only was the Humane Society a force for change, but sentiment about animals in the United States was also changing.

A conservation movement was growing in the country, led partly by President Theodore Roosevelt. While Roosevelt was president, he established several national monuments, numerous bird and animal preserves and 150 national forests. Roosevelt first designated the Hiawatha National Forest in

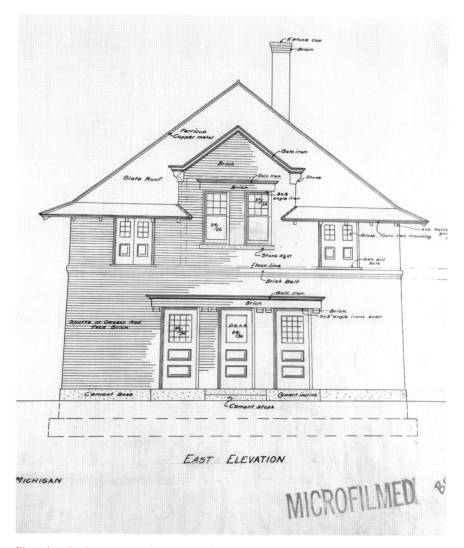

Blueprints for the new pound near the garbage burner on the island. *Grand Rapids City Archives and Records Center.*

the Upper Peninsula as a national forest in 1909. The same year that the pound was exposed, Charles W. Garfield—often called the "first citizen of Grand Rapids"—was compiling a report on forest conservation as president of the State Forestry Commission.

Grand Rapids citizens had become proponents of animal protection. In 1916, when President Woodrow Wilson called on citizens to protect sheep and for the dogs harming them to be destroyed, the editor of the *Herald* excoriated

8

the president, saying, "Why pick on the dogs?"[40] In the 1940s, the citizens of Grand Rapids had an Animal Week, promoting kindness to animals.

In 1949, the care of animals was under the county's authority through a division of the Kent County Health Department. In 1944, the Humane Society built a new facility and offered animal clinics, but in 1960, a devastating fire caused them to relocate. Despite this, stray dogs were still a problem for the city. In the 1970s, the Kent County Animal Control dog warden reported that stray dogs were somewhat owned, meaning that they acquired food and shelter from residents from time to time. He also noted that they had a range of seven to ten city blocks and that in 1977, approximately 10,000 stray animals deposited 2.25 million pounds of fecal matter in the city. It posed a problem to public health. The City Commission recommended that each neighborhood create an animal watch team that would look out for and report on stray animals. In 2001, the Humane Society finished building a new facility on Wilson Drive. The Humane Society continues to facilitate forever homes for animals. In 2016, the Humane Society facilitated the adoption of nearly 3,800 animals. In 2020, a year of relatively few highlights, Paws with a Cause, a nonprofit dedicated to animal adoption, held a socially distanced dog parade for assisted living residents in Grand Rapids.

WHILE DOGS CEASED TO be pests in the eyes of the city, there were still other critters that the city had to contend with and fight against. Grand Rapids adopted a rat bounty, and a pigeon bounty soon followed. In 1885, an almost satirical article graced the pages of the *Grand Rapids Daily Eagle* that relayed a Common Council debate on what to do about sparrows in the city. One alderman recommended sprinkling birdseed on electric wires, hoping the birds would electrocute themselves when they landed for a snack. Another alderman joked that if they would only wait for the next election cycle, all the hot air would just blow the sparrows away. Much to the chagrin of west siders, one alderman suggested herding all the sparrows to the west side.

A bird bounty became the prime solution to deal with the feathery problem. In 1909, the city handsomely paid two cents per sparrow. That year, 10,163 sparrows were caught and brought to city hall. E. Edgerton himself broke a record and brought 612 sparrows to city hall, earning twelve dollars and twenty-four cents. The article about the bird bounty, republished by the Grand Rapids Historical Society in their newsletter, was titled "Boozed Birds Clutter Gutter" and noted that the best way to capture the sparrows was to soak birdseed in whisky.

CHAPTER 6

FEEDING A CITY

E very one must do his damnedest to win the war."[41] The words echoed through the Ryerson Library on March 26, 1918, nearly one year after the United States entered the First World War. Grand Rapids had over one thousand sons fighting overseas, and thousands of women in Kent County signed up for war work with the Council of National Defense. As in nearly every city in the United States, the home front had come to Grand Rapids. As with the conservation of munitions and labor, Grand Rapids also united under the notion that "food will win the war."

Guy Winchester Rouse invited the speaker quoted above to the library and the local grocery retailers gathered to hear how they could aid the war effort. Rouse was named the Kent County food administrator in December 1917, spearheading projects around Grand Rapids aimed at curbing waste and rationing resources.

Rouse's father, William, fought for the Union army during the Civil War, and his ancestor Jonathan Winchester fought against the British. Rouse's strengths lay not on the battlefield but in the analytical field. He worked as a bank auditor until becoming secretary for the Grocery Company. Due to his prowess, he advanced until he became president of the company, leading him to become the prime candidate when Grand Rapids needed a food czar.

Since the war began in 1914, the wider world was experiencing depletion of food supplies. Despite the United States being relatively insulated from shortages outside its border, as early as 1916, reports emerged that the food

City workers and volunteers at the city social at Lyon and Bond. *Grand Rapids City Archives and Records Center.*

shortage was coming to Michigan. A combination of destructive storms, depleted surpluses and labor shortages meant rationing was on its way.

The grocery retailers who came to the library to hear Rouse and his speakers were urged to guide their customers to conserve where they could, substitute where possible and use less flour and sugar. "We should be willing to sacrifice for the good of the whole," Rouse proclaimed, urging his community to ration food.[42]

In 1917, a sugar ration began in Kent County. Residents were allowed to have three pounds of sugar a month, and the ingredient would be sold only on specific dates. When traveling to grocers, housekeepers presented their identification cards, indicating the number of family members they were shopping for. Grocers then marked the card, showing that the sugar had been issued and making it impossible for the housekeeper to go to another grocer to purchase extra sugar and cheat the system.

The *Grand Rapids Press* noted that it was necessary to enact the ration due to some customers and grocers who were not abiding by the informal rules. A grocer at 842 Leonard Street NW was arrested and convicted for selling one hundred pounds of sugar to a single customer. As a penalty, he was required to give twenty-five dollars to the Red Cross. Grocers approved the rationing practice because it took the impetus off them to monitor which customers bought how much sugar. It seemed that women did a large amount of the grocery shopping and were the ones filling out the ration cards. On the whole, Guy W. Rouse noted that the city would follow the rules for the good of the country.

Grand Rapids's history is also a history of food. Food played its part in every structure built and road platted. It nourished the city and helped it grow. From the pure food movement to rationing during World War I, from coffee to restaurants and food trucks, Grand Rapids has a truly unique history of food.

NATIVE AMERICANS ATE FISH and harvested corn around the Grand River Valley. Surveyors noted old Indian fields, as well as wild cherry trees, wild plums and cranberry marshes. Deer and other wild game were prevalent before the advent of white settlers. Wright Coffinberry recounted a hunting excursion he and his neighbors went on in 1858 down the river, where they managed to bag a deer.

Early settlers brought in food sources of their own. Early supplies came from Detroit. When Grand Rapids gained more residents, several farms surrounded the city. In 1860, there were roughly seventy-five farms in Grand Rapids. The first farms grew wheat and corn, but in his *History of Grand Rapids*, Albert Baxter wrote that fruits and vegetables began to dominate the farm scene: "Apples, peaches, pears, plum and cherries, and the berry fruits, and onions, celery, asparagus, beans and peas, and the several root crops."[43]

Food habits of the early city hide in various city records. In the 1859 city directory, there were six bakers, four breweries, three confectioners, three flour mills, one fruit and vegetable seller and already over thirty grocers and several saloons. Baxter notes that pepper and salt were staples in cooking—nothing new there. He also describes how the very early villagers would get their meat. Farmers butchered a cow or lamb and brought the meat into town. They drove wagons through the streets, selling the cuts to passersby. Later, meat markets popped up, the first opening in 1842.

Food was symbolic as well. In 1865, when the nation's president, Abraham Lincoln, was assassinated, Grand Rapids aldermen enacted a citywide day of fasting to mourn the fallen president.

Leonard Street Farmers Market in 1927. *Grand Rapids City Archives and Records Center.*

Sometimes residents were paid for their work in food. For several surveying jobs, Wright Lewis Coffinberry earned pay in the form of food, such as potatoes. Locals also tended gardens. Settler Abel Page raised the first tomatoes in the city. Gardens were valued, and their destruction was a severe offense. In 1874, Cornelius Harvey became a felon for maliciously destroying someone's garden in the city. The same thing happened in 1877, when Frederick Puleson ruined someone's garden. In the early 1910s, a city engineer wrote in his surveying journal that he had paid someone to plant potatoes and grapes along with oats, rye and wheat. In 1873, the total value of garden vegetables and fruit in Grand Rapids was around $3,000, well over $100,000 in today's dollars. Orchards were also popular.

In the 1890s, surveyor Theodore O. Williams jotted notes about his diet in his surveying journal. He noted that he should only eat "fruits, grains, vegetables, butter, eggs, chicken, pork, beef, and fish."[44] He questioned whether or not he should eat mutton. Williams would only allow himself to drink water, tea, milk and sweet wines. He wrote a page in his journal on how to care for chickens and two pages on beekeeping methods. Williams's records provide an example of what the average Grand Rapidian thought about food.

Above: Local grocery store at 610 Alexander Street SE in 1936. *Grand Rapids City Archives and Records Center.*

Left: Local grocery store at 781 College Avenue NE in 1936. *Grand Rapids City Archives and Records Center.*

Grocery stores, meat markets and specialty shops became popular, and almost every street seemed to sport its local grocery store. Wholesale markets arose in the 1870s with the establishment of stalls on Monroe Avenue near Hasting Street. The largest market opened in 1897 on what had been the last island of the city. Grocery store owners knew their neighborhood and likely lived where they worked. They knew their customers, making them able to provide their customers with guidance during rationing. But despite this, occasionally, there were cases where sellers used unscrupulous means to make a profit.

MICHIGAN, AND GRAND RAPIDS, adopted a series of pure food laws to combat untoward food business practices. While the federal government did not adopt the Pure Food and Drug Act until 1906, Michigan passed a pure food law in 1893. The law created the position of dairy and food commissioner. In 1895, an amendment to the Michigan pure food law expanded the food commissioner's authority. In November, the *Grand Rapids Press* noted that the state food commissioner was on his way to Grand Rapids to make war with impure food providers.

The commissioner, Charles E. Storr, was appointed in 1893 by the governor. A resident of Michigan since 1858, Storr had served in the Sixth Michigan Cavalry, organized in Grand Rapids. He lived primarily in Ottawa and Mason Counties. Storr came to Grand Rapids in 1895 with his many inspectors and assistants, looking for food contaminants. His targets were decomposed animals, imitation cheese, milk from diseased cows and rotten food. Also on his chopping block was canned food containing harmful contaminants, vinegar containing lead or copper particles and food labels that did not match the product.

For commissioner Storrs's 1896 annual report, inspectors interviewed several grocers in Grand Rapids to gather insight on how they felt about the law. The consensus seemed to be positive. One grocer stated, "There is a great improvement in the class of food products sold in the State of Michigan," while another noted that "the law is a service to both the dealer and consumer."[45] While the interviewer noted that none of those interviewed spoke ill of the law, one of those interviewed noted that some "unscrupulous parties" were skirting the law.[46] Indeed, the Morse Dry Goods Company on Monroe Center was selling impure brandy. Alois Rasch, the owner of the Staple and Fancy Groceries shop on Monroe Avenue NW, sold coffee beans that were 21 percent roasted peas.

Local inspectors and leaders were also involved in cracking down on impure foods. In 1895, residents complained that milk-providing cows were grazing near the "big ditch." The big ditch, the West Side Ditch, was dug in 1874 to drain sections of the city's west side and provide a sewage outlet. It began near Richmond Street and ran down to the Grand River. A few sewers emptied into the ditch. Residents were concerned that contaminants from the ditch were getting into the milk supply from cows drinking ditchwater. The city leaders ordered the poundmaster to force herders to keep their cows from drinking the water.

By 1900, likely thanks to the pure food inspectors, Grand Rapids had become one of the top cities in the state for pure food. Deputy state food

Department of Weights and Measures staff measuring barrels. *Grand Rapids City Archives and Records Center.*

inspector John R. Bennett stated in the *Grand Rapids Press*, "There are no groceries in the country in better shape than those of Grand Rapids."[47] Despite this high rating, Grand Rapids still had incidents of concern. In 1904, local meat inspectors found that a significant portion of meat sold at the market came from diseased cows, primarily those with tuberculosis.

Local food inspectors of the city's Department of Health did most of the investigative groundwork. Dr. William McLean, the Grand Rapids City milk inspector, uncovered that diseased cows were an ample source of meat supplied to markets. McLean also hosted a milk inspection training at City Hall in 1903 with attendees from as far as Connecticut. In 1902, the milk inspectors' annual report noted that there were 466 licensed milk dealers in the city and that farmers would sell their milk from wagons around the city. The report also stated that staff inspected 3,423 cows for quality. The following year, 4,244 cows were inspected. In 1905, McLean became director of the Department of Milk and Meat Inspection, resulting from his investigative work on the condition of meat.

Condemned meat from the markets would be loaded onto city wagons and brought to the garbage burner. In two days in the summer of 1916, the

Court record for George M. Morse stating that he was arrested for violation of the pure food law in 1902. *Grand Rapids City Archives and Records Center.*

city inspector found 1,500 pounds of tainted meat. The inspector noted in the press that he had never seen so much tainted meat in the city before. He traced the tainted meat back to Fisher Station, a train depot in Kelloggsville. Individuals arrested by pure food agents would be brought to trial. George M. Morse was arrested in 1902 for selling adulterated butter and brought before the police court.

McLean later became a target of malign, for it came out that he was the veterinarian for many milk companies in the city, and there were cries that he was providing preferential treatment. The press mentioned "ugly stories" circulating about the milk inspector, but the informant's name was being kept a secret by committee investigators. The committee investigation uncovered that the "ugly stories" involved reports that the Sanitary Milk Company, for whom McLean was a veterinarian, was allowed to sell impure milk. The inspection uncovered no substantiation to the claims, and the committee asserted that the milk inspector's salary of $900 a year was not enough to support a family. McLean was well within his right to continue his private practice. Despite this, McLean did not stay on as milk inspector, due to the controversy.

Markets and conventions opened in Grand Rapids, showing examples of pure food. The Cherry Farm Dairy company, located on Scribner Street, exhibited milk, butter, cottage cheese and several other dairy products at a pure food show in Grand Rapids in 1904. Along with their wares, the company also brought equipment to show attendees how they processed their milk. "Pure food" soon became a mark of a good product, and advertisers often used it as a slogan.

AROUND THE SAME TIME as the pure food movement, a movement for more measurement oversight arose. Citizens complained to the Common Council in 1903 that the measurement of products sold in the city was not uniform. The council relegated the problem to the Committee on Ways and Means. The committee found that while most businesses were fair, some sold packages with fewer products than advertised or had inaccurate scales. The committee advised that a sealer of weights and measures be appointed to inspect scales around the city. The committee noted, "It is not simply the consumer who is to be protected, but it is a matter of justice to the honorable dealer."[48]

Standard measures approved by the Sealer before being sold to the Public; notice the difference between the three illegal measures and the standard measures.

Comparison of standard measurement containers versus illegal measurement containers. *Grand Rapids City Archives and Records Center.*

Above: 701–5 Division Avenue S, the first store to receive a weights and measures stamp of approval. *Grand Rapids City Archives and Records Center*.

Left: City workers testing gasoline pumps to make sure the correct amount was dispensed. *Grand Rapids City Archives and Records Center*.

The city sealer was appointed to provide his approved seal on packages in the city that adhered to the agreed-upon measurements. Bags of flour were stamped and barrels measured for accuracy. On his first round of inspections, Samuel DeLong inspected eight grocery stores, a few meat markets and a single hardware store. He condemned three sets of scales used to cheat customers out of several ounces of meat per purchase. Lawrence M. Wilson, a grocer at 701–5 Division Avenue S, was the first to receive a stamp of approval on his scales.

Sealer DeLong gave a record of his activities in a report to the City Commission in 1904. He noted that consumers, on average, paid for five quarts per day for a specific product that they did not receive due to faulty scales. This discrepancy amounted to the large sum of $24,414 in lost product for customers per year, a large amount even by today's standards, notwithstanding that the same amount today would be over $700,000. When it came to weighing flour alone, Delong noted that consumers lost $53,532 in total annually.

GRAND RAPIDS'S FOOD IMPROVED during the city's early adoption of pure food regulations and weights and measures inspections. The city banded together to conserve rations during World War I. The Great Depression created another test for Grand Rapids's food production. Poverty rose, and out-of-work men had families to provide for and mouths to feed.

During the First World War, labor was at a premium. Workers were needed so badly that college students ineligible for the draft suspended their studies to become farm laborers to help the cause. Sixty-eight Calvin College boys volunteered to travel to various farms around the country. The Great Depression caused the opposite problem. Hundreds of men sought work.

The Grand Rapids Public Welfare Department was created in earnest in 1918 to provide aid during World War I. The first year the department was organized, Fred Locke oversaw its activities, which the *Grand Rapids Press* said was "Hooverizing"—meaning, at that time, to save and be sparing with food supplies. Locke printed menus that bore the title "The Necessity of Patriotism" and handed them out to families that received food aid. The menus provided families with instructions on how to preserve food. That first year, $18,374 worth of groceries went to needy families. Beans, pork, sugar and rice were among the supplies received by needy families. The department even started delivering groceries to families whose mothers could not leave children alone or were too infirm to leave the house.

COMMODITIES DISBURSED FROM SOCIAL SERVICE DIVISION

YEAR 1918-1919

COMMODITY	AMOUNT DISBURSED DURING YEAR
Baking Powder	327-cans
Beans	2994-#
Carrots	4925-#
Cocoa	707-#
Codfish	1040-#
Coffee	1371-#
Cornmeal	5329-#
Eggs	829-Dozen
Wheat Flour	32631-#
Graham Flour	1315-#
Rye Flour	2051-#
Lard Compound	2484-#
Macaroni	1888-#
Matches	1862-Bxs.
Salt Pork	340½-#
Fresh Meat	1129-#
Milk	87453-Pints
Oleomargarine	4523-#
Onions	4981-#
Peas	2762-#
Potatoes	47675-#
Prunes	3946-#
Rice	3367-#
Rolled Oats	6369-#
Salt	1500-#
Soap	7184-Bars
Starch	289-#
Sugar	4486-#
Syrup	1891-cans
Tea	407-#
Turnips	3218-#
Barley	858-#
Barley Flour	3550-#
Corn Flour	3100-#
Cream of Wheat	4-Pkgs
Yeast	6-Pkgs
Dried Apples	17-#
Hard Coal	14-Tons
Soft Coal	351¾-Tons
Coke	84-Tons
Wood	625½-Cords
Shoes	573-Pairs
Rubbers	10-Pairs

List of food distributed by the Social Services Division from mid-1918 to mid-1919. *Grand Rapids City Archives and Records Center.*

Locke eventually impressed the city with his managerial skills and became city manager. A man named A.E. Davidson took over as director of the Department of Social Welfare, and the Social Services Department became a division under the management of Edith Dykema, one of the first women to head a division or department within the city.

Edith was born in Michigan in 1886 and graduated from the Chicago School of Civics and Philanthropy. Edith signed up when the Council of National Defense's Women's Committee was registering women for war service. The committee interviewer noted that Edith was in good health, wore glasses and was unmarried. She was thirty-two at the time and worked for the Social Welfare Association, a nonprofit in the city. Edith noted that she had experience with accounting, sewing and work as a librarian and that she wanted to stay within the city.

Under Edith Dykema, 1,594 families were given material aid by the Social Services Division; 247 families received groceries for at least six months. In all, $15,516 went to groceries for families. Edith's annual report, only the second for the Social Services Division, started the practice of listing foods that would be provided to families. These included vegetables such as carrots, onions, potatoes and turnips. Dried apples were provided as well. Things like macaroni, eggs, cornmeal and even fish were listed.

Throughout 1928, before the economic collapse, only 385 families needed provisions. By the following year, unemployment had reached a peak. Guy E. Northrup, the new manager of the Social Services Division, noted that the year saw the most considerable amount of food ever provided. Over five hundred families received at least some groceries to make it through the year. The following year, those numbers again jumped.

The social services department began operating a City Social Center at 58 Commerce Avenue. There, transient men looking for work could find a meal and a place to stay. Truckloads of potatoes would arrive at the social services store, where families could exchange scrip for desperately needed food. In 1931, Northrup created a program where social service workers, some themselves working for scrip, would travel through the city collecting materials for the needy. "Let others use what you aren't using." The signs and banners were plastered in shop windows and on the sides of trucks picking up supplies.

The community banded together; while men sought work building public projects, women volunteered at the Social Services Department, peeling potatoes and measuring out cans of beans and other foods to help a hungry city. Despite the overwhelming surge of support, some did

Women volunteers peeling potatoes at the social services store in 1931. *Grand Rapids City Archives and Records Center.*

Volunteers unloading apples from vehicles sporting the signs "let others use what you aren't using." *Grand Rapids City Archives and Records Center.*

not like the Social Services Division. One uncouth man did not like that women were working in the department. He demanded that the City Commission "discharge the hard boiled women working in your social welfare department"; they had disregarded his request for food, he said, and he had "already requested your City Manager to discharge these hard boiled critters."[49]

A controversy arose when the Social Services Division devised a plan to have milk freely available on a first-come-first-served basis at fire stations around the city. The milk dealers of the city cried foul, saying that the program would hurt their business interests.

WHAT WOULD GRAND RAPIDS be without fruit? A substantial orchard grew on the grounds of the sewage treatment plant in 1934. Red Delicious, McIntosh, Golden Delicious, Bartlett pears, Italian prune plums and even apricots grew. In total, there were 242 trees. The orchard was just one manifestation of the art of pomology that was prominent in Grand Rapids.

In 1871, the Michigan legislature passed an act that allowed societies to incorporate to promote pomology, the science of fruit. Citizens in and around Grand Rapids formed the Grand River Valley Horticultural Society to encourage pomology. At their first meeting, a member read an essay titled "How to Pick and Pack Apples, and Where to Keep Them, and Where to Sell Them," as well as a lecture titled "Grape Culture."[50] Grand Rapids eventually became one of the state's best fruit-growing regions. One of the society's later members became a champion of pomology and nature. His name was Charles Garfield.

Charles Garfield was friendly with a grape grower in Grand Rapids near the corner of Knapp and Plainfield. William K. Munson grew what he called the King Grape. The large blue grape became renowned in pomology circles, largely due to Charles Garfield's promotion. When judges of the American Pomological Association dismissed the grape as an old variety, Garfield spent eight years convincing them that the King Grape was indeed a distinct type of grape, a new variety. The King Grape won a bronze medal reserved for individuals from the American Pomological Association when they conceded that it was indeed a new kind of grape grown exclusively in Grand Rapids. Garfield noted that Grand Rapids men had traveled through the United States, attending pomological society meetings and promoting the prominent fruit grown in West Michigan.

In 1922, Kent County fruit farmers agreed to move their products solely through the Grand Rapids Grower's Association in the hopes that the centralization would improve their profits. The association had already done something similar for tomato growers in Grand Rapids, and those farmers said that the plan allowed them to market their produce farther than Michigan's borders.

THE HISTORY OF RESTAURANTS in Grand Rapids is well documented in Norma Lewis's book *Lost Restaurants of Grand Rapids*. From early hotels serving food to saloons and bars downtown, Lewis recounts the delights of having a meal downtown. It is still a treat to visit one of the many great eateries in Grand Rapids.

On the periphery is the history of coffee in Grand Rapids. The dark drink delivering essential caffeine is one of Grand Rapids's favorite drinks. Louis Campau and other early settlers had coffee and would share it with guests. Saloons and restaurants served coffee, and residents who could afford it had coffee at home. In 1900, the *Grand Rapids Press* wrote an article about the

Front Avenue location for the Ferris Coffee and Nut Co., circa 1970. *Grand Rapids City Archives and Records Center*.

art of serving coffee. "What does one wish to express in serving a cup of coffee to a friend?" the article asked. Coffee should be served fresh for every occasion, it said, and if the homeowner could not devote one whole room to coffee serving, a corner in a large drawing room would suffice. The article ended by exclaiming that he who masters the art of serving coffee masters the art of living.[51]

The Pantlind hotel served coffee for thirty cents a cup. An early local chain café, called the Coffee Ranch, was located at 24 Division Avenue N, just a few stores down from the Civic Theater. There, you could get two pounds of coffee for sixty-three cents. The shop, run by Carl Hoffman, was originally located on Monroe Center in the early 1910s, and Hoffman advertised that the coffee was roasted the same day customers purchased it.

It was Ferris Coffee and Nut Company, however, that made a lasting impact. There were, in fact, earlier coffee roasters in the city. Wilber F. Dickerson was listed as a coffee roaster on Monroe Avenue in the 1886 city directory. Hallett B. Hayward worked as a coffee roaster for the Worden Grocer Co. in 1912. In 1901, John Caulfield noted that he was ramping up a new coffee-roasting operation on Ottawa Avenue S, working under the name of Home Mills Coffee & Spice Co. Another, known as the F.M.C. Coffee Mills, operated on the corner of Louis and Campau Streets, roughly where Z's Bar and Restaurant is now. Several small roasters popped up here and there, but none have had the lasting power of Ferris.

Ferris has a more extended history than many realize. Jay Floyd Ferris moved to Grand Rapids in 1881 and opened a New York Tea Co. on Monroe Center. In 1904, the name changed to Ferris, and Jay's son William took over the company's operation. When William retired in 1913, the coffee shop was purchased by Stuart F. Johnson. It was at this time that Ferris started a coffee delivery service. The company also opened a Ferris Coffee Ranch at 936–38 Division Avenue S. There is some evidence that they named their coffee flavors after streets in the city. One *Grand Rapid Press* article notes that a blend they sold was the Ferris Fulton Park Coffee blend, available for thirty cents. In 1924, the company was again sold to brothers Herman and Ray Wierenga. They opened the Ferris Coffee and Nut Co. on Front Street on the west side, the side of the river they have operated out of ever since.

Many roasters and coffee shops have joined Ferris: Schuil Coffee Co., MadCap, Roots Coffee Co., Rowster's Coffee and many others. Coffee shops have become staples of the community, like the Bitter End Coffee House and Common Ground, PaLatte Coffee and Art, Lantern Coffee Bar and Lounge, Lyon Street Café and the Sparrows. The energizing beverage gives residents and visitors the jolt they need to thrive.

Grand Rapids would not be the city it is today without coffee, nor without its food history. Food sustains the city, and the city thoroughly enjoys its food. Grand Rapids excelled at food rationing, protecting consumers and providing for its many hungry residents.

CHAPTER 7

CRIMINAL ELEMENT

John Leonard was arrested on January 14, 1914, by two Grand Rapids Police Department detectives. Wearing a suit and tie, sporting clean-cut hair and a well-maintained mustache, he did not look the part of a hardened criminal. Leonard carried himself with authority and was well-spoken. Those who interacted with him, taking in his intense blue eyes, thought that he was someone of import.

The detectives were searching specifically for Leonard that Wednesday afternoon. Earlier in the day, Leonard had passed a worthless forged check for thirty-five dollars at the A. May and Son's clothing store, located at the corner of Monroe and Lyon. The store was managed by Meyer May at the time, famous now for his home designed by Frank Lloyd Wright. May noticed that his clerk had accepted the bogus check; seeing it was from a bank in Wyandotte, Michigan, he notified the police. May's affluent status in the city might have caused the police to exercise their full investigative powers.

It was actually by chance that Leonard was located. He happened to be passing another forged check at the Wepman clothing store at 119 Division Avenue S at the same time the detectives walked through the door. Leonard, seeing the officers, attempted to draw a .32 automatic revolver from his jacket. Before he could let off a shot, officers pushed him to the floor.

After Leonard's arrest, officers searched his hotel room. He had been staying at either the Irving or the Stokes Hotel; the newspapers mention only that it was the corner of Division and Weston. Officers found an immense quantity of blank checks, money orders from Wells Fargo and a complete

Mug shots for John M. Leonard, arrested in 1914. *Grand Rapids City Archives and Records Center.*

book of blank money orders from the Fishkill Post Office in New York State. Several rubber stamps rounded out Leonard's forging supplies to fill his checks and money orders. In his jacket, he also carried more than $350, which back then amounted to nearly $10,000 today.

John Leonard was an enigma to officers and the newspapers covering him. He gave several aliases when arrested, claiming he was M.J. Reece or E.A. Carter. The *Grand Rapids Herald* referred to him as Reece, as did the *Grand Rapids Press*. Leonard refused to sign his name on the fingerprint card file the police department filled out about their detained offender. The police department notified federal authorities that they had a mysterious forger on their hands, thinking that he might be wanted elsewhere based on the evidence of his stolen checks and money orders.

Leonard sat in the Grand Rapids jail, awaiting word from the feds. A reporter for the *Grand Rapids Press* came to interview the forger. Leonard took the opportunity to come clean about his history. He admitted that his real name was George F. Rose, and he was the son of a wealthy family from Chicago. He claimed he studied law at Northwestern University and had also trained for the seminary for a time. It was a head injury from falling off a horse that caused his personality to alter, inclining him to careen into a life of crime. He proved this last bit by showing the reporter a dent in his head. In the era of phrenology, the reporter was inclined to believe him.

Leonard also mentioned that he had spent time in federal prison. This revelation was, in fact, true. The record that the police uncovered showed that he had been arrested multiple times for forgery and burglary. His arrest record and newspapers from around the country show his magnificently crafty criminal career.

Leonard's known record started in 1903 in Kalamazoo, Michigan. The charge that officers picked him and a young accomplice up for was carrying a concealed weapon. The youth, an eighteen-year-old named John King, could not handle the pressure and immediately confessed to no less than eighteen burglaries the two had committed. While Leonard remained silent, John King admitted they had planned two more robberies, one of which, in Augusta, was to happen the next day. The most recent theft was in Baldwin, Michigan, but the *Kalamazoo Gazette* listed their other exploits: a jewelry store robbery in Big Rapids, theft of coal from a Grand Rapids office, theft from a hardware store in Lansing, Carson City depot thievery, stealing from saloons and homes. They even stole a golden urn from a Catholic church in Reed City.

Once Leonard was placed in the county jail, he became more eloquent and began to regale officers with his exploits, including a primer on how to blow safe doors apart. While Leonard was nonchalant in describing his crimes, King was not handling it well. He blamed the older criminal for leading him into this life and said that the older man forced him to do much of the actual thievery. "He treated me like a dog," the young man exclaimed, tears running down his face. "It's an awful feeling to know that you are guilty."[52]

Leonard demanded a jury trial, likely believing he could count on his guile and charm to escape justice. John King, whose actual name was Ed Quinn, was transferred to Grand Haven to answer for his burglary there. While in transit through Grand Rapids, the youth slipped from his bonds and fled, ultimately escaping justice.

Leonard entered recorder's court in November 1903, acting as his own attorney. The jury and reporters noted that he must have been an able lawyer in a past life, for he was well versed in legal acumen and precedents. He cross-examined witnesses himself and was said to be quite clever for a burglar. The *Kalamazoo Gazette* even noted that the judge sustained many of Leonard's objections during the plaintiff's questioning. During the trial, Leonard's background as a Northwestern graduate was discussed, and Leonard even mentioned he had been a prosecuting attorney in Illinois. Despite his valiant attempt, Leonard was sentenced to ninety days in the county jail, after which he would be tried for his most recent burglary in Baldwin.

For that crime, Leonard received ten years in Jackson Prison; he was forty-one at the time. An article in the *Evening Press* in Grand Rapids noted that he had already spent sixteen years of his life in various prisons for various crimes, but his official record does not provide details. While awaiting transfer to Jackson, Leonard attempted to cut through the bars of his cell with a hacksaw he had sewn into his pants. All the while, he was still bragging about his audacious life. The *Kalamazoo Gazette* wrote that apart from being a burglar and a lawyer, he was also a practiced stenographer and bookkeeper.

What is extraordinary is that while in prison, John Leonard had enough legal acumen to appeal his case to the Michigan Supreme Court, acting as his own lawyer the whole way. Leonard argued that the maximum sentence should not have been more than one year due to new state law. The supreme court did not agree, and Leonard stayed in Jackson Prison until 1907, when he was transferred up north to Marquette. He remained in Marquette until 1911, when he received a conditional pardon from the governor of Michigan.

Leonard made his way to Chicago, Illinois, where he was subsequently arrested in January 1923 for attempting to pass a forged check. While held by Chicago authorities, he told his captors that he had escaped from Marquette, but there is no evidence that this was true. Leonard was sentenced to five years in the United States Penitentiary, Leavenworth, in Kansas. While there, he successfully submitted an appeal that he was, in fact, insane and should be transferred to an insane asylum in Washington, D.C.

In transit to the insane asylum, John Leonard escaped. He was apprehended in Chester, Pennsylvania, in December 1913, attempting to use more counterfeit money to purchase tobacco. He had been arrested with a fellow convict, an African American man named John Howard, and both were locked in the police station. This time, Leonard relayed that he had been a practicing attorney from Detroit and had married an extremely wealthy society woman in that city. An inattentive guard accidentally forgot to lock the cell door, and like a scene in a movie, Leonard donned a coat and hat he found in the offices and walked calmly out of jail in his disguise. John Howard was not so fortunate and remained in custody. After some prodding, he relayed that the two convicts had walked from Washington to Baltimore and, from there, fallen in with a band of highway robbers.

The Philadelphia news also relayed that Leonard had married in Michigan but was soon divorced when the woman realized his charm had fooled her. There is little evidence of this, however. Leonard might have used an altogether unknown alias for his marriage, if there was one. It is possible that years were jumbled in Leonard's tales. In 1908, the *Flint Journal* noted that a man named John Leonard had seduced a married woman. The townspeople hung an effigy of Leonard from a light post and labeled him a homewrecker. This Leonard was forced to defend himself from an irate husband and, in the subsequent court troubles, happened to represent himself, acting as his own lawyer. The *Grand Rapids Press* article published about his exploits in 1914 says that he had been married but had been arrested in Detroit for attempting to kill a man for breaking up his family. For this version of the story to be accurate or half true, Leonard would have to have been paroled earlier than his record states—or actually broken out of jail, as an earlier record stated.

While he sat in the Grand Rapids jail cell in 1914, after nearly a decade of daring criminal exploits, Leonard recounted wild tales to the *Grand Rapids Press* reporter. He claimed he had pleaded his case directly to the governor, which secured his release, along with that of 172 other convicts. Time and memory may have altered some of the details. The single press article found about a slew of Marquette pardons in 1911 stated that sixty individuals were pardoned; John Leonard was likely just one of those lucky few. Regardless of the truth or lack thereof, the *Grand Rapids Press* painted a romantic picture of this man. The problem was that the man arrested for forgery had forged his entire background.

His name was not John M. Leonard, George F. Rose or one of the myriad of others he used throughout his life of crime. It was Edwin VanMeter. He was not a lawyer, did not attend Northwestern and had not even grown up in the Midwest. He was born in Petersburg, Virginia, and employed as a cobbler, like his father. His Jackson and Marquette Prison records shed some light on his true persona. His mother had died when he was young, and his father, George, still resided in Petersburg.

"Leonard" was sent back to the Leavenworth penitentiary, serving the remainder of his sentence there until he was removed in 1916 to answer for crimes in New York, specifically for robbing that Fishkill post office. His story picks back up many years later when his obituary was published in 1958 in Virginia. It lists his father's and mother's names, corroborated by prison records. The most surprising thing, in the end, was that he seemed to have settled down. He had married; fathered a son, whom he named Edwin; and had actually practiced law in Virginia after his life of crime.

THE MUG SHOTS, FINGERPRINTS and court records stored at the Grand Rapids Public Museum and the Grand Rapids City Archives and Records Center, shed light on unimaginably fascinating stories—human stories. They provide insight into a segment of the population rarely explored in historical narratives. The criminal entries show where individuals were born, sometimes providing information on their profession. Immigration, Prohibition and other subjects of interest, like the outlandish account of Leonard, are only the tip of the iceberg regarding the wealth of information found within the records.

CHAPTER 8

LOST ART

In 1976, Nancy Mulnix, Stuart O. Dawson and William Pries presided over a competition for the Festival of the Arts. They gathered to inspect several models three months before the festival began, each using their expertise to judge which would win. Nancy Mulnix was well known in the city for championing the acquisition of *La Grande Vitesse*. This Alexander Calder sculpture has dominated imagery of the city since its addition to the city landscape. Stuart Dawson was an architect specializing in landscapes, in town for the festival but also because his company, Sasaki Associates, was involved with designing and building Ah-Nab-Awen Park. William Pries was the Grand Rapids Parks Department director who had been instrumental in turning Monroe Center into a pedestrian mall earlier in the decade.

The group gathered to judge sculptures submitted for the Festival of the Arts playground sculpture contest. Contestants entered forty-eight models, and some had come from as far away as Maryland. All the entries lay spread out on a few folding tables. The *Grand Rapids Press* noted there were oversized letters, tubes, wooden mazes and other fun-shaped objects among the entries.

One sculpture caught the judges' attention above the rest: a large red button. The button was as of yet unnamed, and the model included stitching through the buttonholes. The artist was Hy Zelkowitz, a native of New York City who had moved to the Grand Rapids area a few years prior. He won $500 for his sculpture and eventually named the piece *Lorrie's Button*.

Lorrie's Button at its new home in Ah-Nab-Awen Park. *Grand Rapids City Archives and Records Center.*

The large red button can still be found and climbed on today in Ah-Nab-Awen Park. It moved to the park a few weeks after the festival ended. It had stayed in Calder Plaza for several weeks following the Festival of the Arts, where it debuted to the public. Children were encouraged to play on the art installation. City workers have recently repaired its fiberglass exterior after it served as a mode of joy for children for over thirty years. Zelkowitz imagined his button as a link between past and present, stitching two time periods together. Construction of the button took place during the bicentennial, America's celebration of the previous two hundred years. When he won the contest, Zelkowitz stated, "The Bicentennial is a time to rediscover that our country is not the product of spasmodic movements, not separate chapters in history text, but rather a continuum of effort that has progressed from its conception."[53]

Lorrie's Button is just one expression of the continuum of public art that Grand Rapids exhibits. While the red Calder stabile ushered in a new era in public art in the city, public sculptures echo back to the early days of the city. Early citizens banded together to fund elaborate fountains in Veterans Memorial Park and Crescent Park. Loraine Pratt Immen donated bronze busts. War memorials and sculptures that evoke a sense of grandeur and appreciation adorn parks throughout the city. Ironically, the *Grand Rapids Press* wrote in 1909, "Grand Rapids has never been noted as a city of art loving people."[54] The city is known worldwide as a paramount art hub.

Grand Rapids's early public art was, in some sense, utilitarian. Early fountains placed in Crescent Park and Veterans Memorial Park, sculptures like that of Longfellow and monuments like the Civil War memorial were meant to pay homage, erected as specific tributes. In *History of Grand Rapids*, Baxter starts his chapter on art with photography. He includes a section on painting but provides no full biographies of painters. Aaron B. Turner, known for his famous painting of early Grand Rapids, is mentioned only regarding his public career. He was the first city clerk and was appointed postmaster by Ulysses S. Grant. While this oversight likely may be because Turner turned to art later in life, it is still indicative of the relatively little importance painting had in early Grand Rapids history.

While art increased exponentially in the 1970s, Grand Rapids had a slew of prominent painters throughout the preceding decades. Individuals like Sarah Nelson, Mathias Alten, Frederick Stuart Church, Lawrence Earle, Alexander Flyn and Orville Bulman gained recognition for their paintings. The Grand Rapids Historical Commission documented these artists in detail, and their work is found in the myriad of institutions in town dedicated to preserving art.

While some of the paintings by these individuals immortalize Grand Rapids topics, many depict topics that transcend the city. Because of this, the artworks themselves may be divorced, to a degree, from the city of their artist. Public sculptures, however, must, by their geographic position, be seen in the context of the city. *La Grande Vitesse* must be viewed in person within Grand Rapids; it can be experienced in full by an admirer whose feet are firmly planted in the plaza in which it sits. You cannot view the Calder without seeing past it toward some aspect of the cityscape.

In 1973, a downtown-wide exhibit opened to showcase sculptures. The exhibit, "Sculpture Off the Pedestal," was the Art Prize competition of its day. It is safe to say that Art Prize, the world-renowned art competition that began in 2009, would not exist had there not first been "Sculpture Off the Pedestal." An article in the *Flint Journal* summarized exactly what made the exhibit so special and caused the art community to turn its eye toward Grand Rapids: "The notion that three-dimensional art can come 'off the pedestal' to enrich the lives of ordinary folks."[55] The exhibit inspired other cities to attempt the same, such as an exhibit of eleven sculptures in Houston, Texas, that the *Houston Chronicle* admitted was a spiritual successor to the Grand Rapids exhibit.

The twelve sculptures that graced the Grand Rapids downtown area were successful due to the efforts of the Women's Committee of the Grand Rapids Art Museum and a grant from the National Endowment for the Arts. Most of the artwork was temporary, such as Mark di Suvero's *Are Years What?* sculpture of bright red steel I-beams. Some of the pieces inspired Grand Rapids leaders to see the value in public sculptures and procure some permanently. Mark di Suvero was commissioned to manufacture *Motu Viget*, better known as the tire swing sculpture, for the grounds of the Federal Building. Some of the artwork has stayed in the area since the exhibit ended. One such piece that has stayed was titled *Split Ring*, which was a staple of Woodland Mall for nearly forty years before returning to its home downtown in 2016. *Split Ring* was created by artist Clement Meadmore, who passed away in 2005. Some art installations, like *Split Ring*, are instantly recognizable, while some are hidden in plain sight.

Robert Morris's *Project X*, also known as the Earthwork Project, is best seen from far above. An immense crisscrossed walkway of concrete on Belknap Hill, *Project X* can be missed entirely by those walking the paths. Morris's concrete Earthwork project still resides in the park, albeit with a few more cracks that reveal its age.

The Belknap hill area had, for a long time, been in disarray. One map, well known for gracing the inside covers of Z.Z. Lydens's *History of Grand Rapids*, provides a rendering of the original shape of the hill. Coldbrook Creek to the north marked the end of the hill, while the top was sandy, and sources said that the hill's plateau was 160 feet above the level of the river. In the early village days, a cemetery was situated on the hill's northern end. The cemetery was used sparingly, and eventually, the bodies buried on the hill were moved to other cemeteries in the city, most being moved to Fulton Street Cemetery. The cemetery sat where the tennis and pickleball courts are today, with matches unknowingly held on hallowed ground.

The area has seen many phases of development over the years. Some sources recount that dirt was hauled away to fill lowlands and channels. Work started in earnest to turn the land into a park during the Great Depression. As part of a public works project, beginning in the 1930s, unemployed men were hired to dig away at the uneven ground to make the land a suitable place to take a pleasant stroll or drive. The city used scrip labor to tame the rugged, sandy landscape and carved the plateau into much-desired scenery. A small road off Division Avenue entered the park, and residents could drive up and take in the view. While the city was deciding what to do with the hilly land, a sports arena was proposed, complete with circular bleachers and a baseball field. This proposition was debated for some time but ended up going nowhere. Robert Morris's *X* was a welcome walkway addition to the park in the 1970s, later to be joined by other amenities, such as the tennis courts.

PUBLIC SCULPTURES BECAME A hit after Calder and the "Sculpture Off the Pedestal" events. The playground sculpture contest garnered more attention and undoubtedly placed more public art throughout a wider stretch of the city in a short amount of time than anything before it. The "Sculpture Off the Pedestal" festivities came close, though its twelve art installations were centered downtown. The playground sculpture contest was also unique due to its draw for children. Meant to be played on and experienced tactilely by the younger generation, it deserves to have its historical account explored. The first sculpture was a series of wood pylons of varying heights, allowing children to climb and jump from pillar to pillar. This sculpture was followed by a similar piece made of concrete. *Timber Forms* and *Concrete Forms* were the first two sculptures' dull-sounding names, dubbed after the materials from which they were crafted. They were both placed toward the city's northern end in Riverside Park. These works of art must have delighted children for many years. They, however, were eventually lost to time, either removed due to damage or just replaced with upgraded playground equipment. It is easy to imagine that after time passed, the pieces resembled worn-down playground equipment, not the works of art they were, and workers, none the wiser, removed them. Despite their popularity, many of the sculptures have disappeared, possibly in this manner.

In 1973, five separate sculptures by the artist and graduate of Aquinas College Tom Leech were picked to entertain children on Calder Plaza. The sculptures were somewhat abstract but also resembled animals, hence the name *Animal Forms*. These roughly three-hundred-pound, pastel-colored metal creatures eventually found their home in John Ball Park. They also suffered from the sands of time, worn down and finally removed.

Shapes that were simple—like triangles, squares and blocks—yet whimsically designed were often picked as public art pieces. Local companies often donated the materials needed to construct the sculptures. The earlier

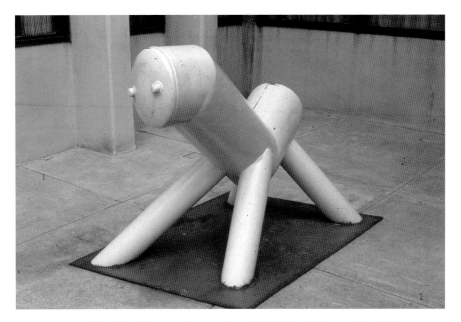

One example of the *Animal Forms* sculptures. *Grand Rapids City Archives and Records Center.*

artists actually spent their earnings paying for the materials needed to turn their models into reality. In 1974, a series of three triangular metal pieces was joined together by metal rods, known as the *Recreform*. The sculpture, a mix of red, purple and yellow-orange set in sand, was sculpted by Mary Garner Preminger. Preminger was born in Grand Rapids in 1920 before moving to New York City to become a renowned fashion model. Eventually, she turned to art and sculpture and returned to Grand Rapids.

The Grand Rapids *Recreform* was not the only one to bear that name. Preminger's sculptures have been played on by children in New York City, San Diego and Grand Rapids. Despite Preminger's fame and the widespread use of her sculptures, the Grand Rapids *Recreform*, sometimes called the Pyramids for its triangular shape, has disappeared.

Luckily, one playground sculpture from 1975 survives in Sixth Street Park, albeit painted a different color. Now red, reminiscent of the Calder, the sculpture called *Kid Katwalk* is a jumble of metal beams jutting out this way and that, allowing youths to practice their balancing skills. Joseph E. Kinnebrew IV designed the delightfully abstract art installation, the same artist we have to thank for the *Fishladder*. His two artworks, among many found in the city, almost kitty-corner to each other across the river, still stand. While one is far more well known, *Kid Katwalk* had more than forty years

Kid Katwalk sculpture. *Grand Rapids City Archives and Records Center.*

of residency in Sixth Street Park. Perhaps the artwork's abstract look has distinguished it as not solely a piece of playground equipment.

After *Kid Katwalk*, the contest became open to the broader public, and after local Hy Zelkowitz won in 1976, another local artist, Robbin Crawford, won the competition in 1977. Another missing piece of art, his large yellow-orange domino sculpture toppled some time ago. The work was titled *Orange-Ganic Domino*, and it was picked out of a lineup of twenty-seven total submissions. The artist carved large holes in the side of the piece, enabling children to crawl through from one side to the other. Two sets of ladders clung to the side of the work to allow kids to climb to the top. In total, the piece weighed 2,600 pounds and was placed briefly in front of the Federal Building before being relocated to another playground and then removed altogether. Sadly, this sculpture was a target for large amounts of graffiti over the years.

The 1978 sculpture piece, also lost to time, was known as *Earth Loops*. Designed and built in 1978 by Robin Jenson, an art professor at Calvin College, the piece resembled a serpent looping in and out of the earth as though it were water. The sculpture was followed in 1979 by *Split*, a ramp-like sculpture made of segmented wood designed by James Kuiper. *Split* was eventually moved to Mulick Park, but like many of the sculptures, it was ultimately removed.

Orange-Ganic Domino sculpture, having been graffitied. *Grand Rapids City Archives and Records Center.*

Ah-Nab-Awen Park and Sixth Street Park have the last two playground sculptures. Solely for the enjoyment of parkgoers and a feature of the first few inaugural years of the Festival of the Arts, these sculptures must have brought memories back to all who played on them. Whether the missing sculptures were removed due to disrepair or to make room for updated playground equipment, they live on through the historical record. Nine playground sculptures in total were donated to the city in the span of nine years.

THE FESTIVAL OF THE ARTS was the catalyst that kicked off both the "Sculpture Off the Pedestal" exhibit and the playground sculpture contest. The Municipal Art Advisory Commission was instrumental in organizing and implementing arts policies. The commission was provided a stipend for every festival to purchase art from festival artists. The city became a unique art collector, gathering submissions from mainly local artists. Much of that artwork graces the walls throughout city offices.

The city purchased works in many mediums: acrylic on paper, oil on canvas, photo etching and myriad others. In 1978, the Art Advisory Commission published a pamphlet listing the art purchased and displayed thus far. Of the fifty artworks listed, thirty-three originated from Grand Rapids artists, thirteen came from artists around Michigan and the rest came from around the country. Because the bulk of the artwork came from local artists, the collection, still found throughout City Hall, is an abstract representation of the city. Appropriately, the pamphlet began with an introduction from the commission, beginning with: "Art reflects mankind. It emphasizes our strengths and reveals our weaknesses."[56]

The art in Grand Rapids reflects the people within. Whether an abstract sculpture meant for the enjoyment of playground children or an ornate monument dedicated to a specific aspect of the city's history, art mirrors the populace and inspires them.

CHAPTER 9

EPILOGUE

In 1842, or possibly the year after, Wright Lewis Coffinberry walked down Division Avenue and passed the corner of Division and Fulton. It was early in the morning. Perhaps he was on his way to his watch repair shop. He happened to run into Louis Campau. Coffinberry called him Uncle Louis, like many citizens did during those years. Campau and several other men were digging a large hole in the corner of the intersection, and as Coffinberry looked on, they removed an old quarter section post, most likely of wood, replacing it with a new post, likely also made of wood. The men Campau was with then placed an immense boulder to mark where the lot's corner was located. Campau told Coffinberry that he had removed and replaced the stake multiple times.

One of the first things that Wright Lewis Coffinberry did just over ten years later, when he was elected city surveyor of the newly incorporated city, was replace the wooden stake and the large boulder. Coffinberry this time sunk an iron stake, two and a half feet long, into the lot's ground. Coffinberry saw the stakes as monuments to those that had come before, meaningful totems throughout the city. Coffinberry replaced these wood and stone monuments all over the city, often with iron, creating new monuments. He would replace the monuments that previous surveyors set.

In 1865, Coffinberry placed a large boulder kitty-corner to the spot he had watched Campau put his. The *Grand Rapids Press* noted that the boulder, with a small metal bolt inserted into the granite, was not noticed by many. The monument was hidden in plain sight. This boulder was the benchmark mentioned in the first chapter, the singular place all streets would be measured against.

Photograph of an elderly Wright L. Coffinberry. *Wright L. Coffinberry Papers, 49-s, Coffinberry, Wright L., Bentley Historical Library, University of Michigan.*

Like this hidden monument related to all streets in the city, the tales within this narrative attempt to explain the history of hidden things, often seen but rarely understood: dams and bridges, food and animals, the very maps and building blocks of the city, the humanity that affects all and the information preserved in a record of crime. All hidden, but all present.

Coffinberry's boulder was, like Campau's, eventually removed. In 1913, it was unearthed by Charles A. Houser, who had a contract for setting a concrete foundation for a weather kiosk in Monument Park. While noteworthy for a time, the kiosk, too, was removed in 1921. The stone and iron monument, one of which Coffinberry was so proud, which stood for fifty-eight years, was replaced without much fanfare.

Changes like this are often hidden. Often, the understanding of historical significance is assigned far after the fact, especially to the mundane yet important. Things are not, speaking metaphorically, set in stone in the city. Buildings come and go; organizations organize and disband; people live their lives and pass on to the next. While it is tempting and sometimes appropriate to mourn the past, it is far more important to acknowledge and try to understand it.

Coffinberry was a student of history. He was an ardent supporter of the local lyceum, the precursor to the Grand Rapids Public Museum. He studied

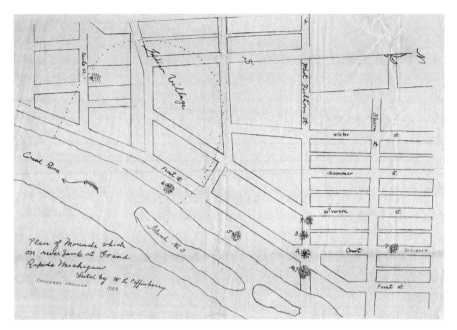

Map of the mounds on the bank of the Grand River, sketched by Wright L. Coffinberry. *Grand Rapids City Archives and Records Center.*

the history and artifacts of Native Americans, attempting to preserve their history. In 1885, four years before he passed away, he sketched a map of the west side of Grand Rapids showing their mounds and the location of the old Native American village.

Coffinberry lived to eighty-two, having spent the second half of his life in service to the city. He worked until he died. It was at six thirty in the morning, on the Grandville Avenue line of the street cable car, on his way to wrap up his job as superintendent of the poor. He had run the department that oversaw aid given to those in need for the last eight years, and he saw no reason to stop on account of his poor health. But his family convinced him to at last retire a few months after a minor stroke.

Coffinberry suffered a second stroke there on the cable car, the only passenger left aboard, falling over just as he reached his stop. The *Evening Leader* remembered him as "genial, honest, upright" and a "scientific character," honoring the old surveyor's life.[57] Coffinberry's mark, his legacy, is hidden in the face of Grand Rapids. Coffinberry knew the value of documenting history and preserving what was lost. Often in the course of history, the new replaces the old. While lamenting these changes is sometimes appropriate, they are often the nature of time. The city is meant to change, adapt, to grow.

Notes

Introduction

1. "Bust and Fountain Formally Presented," *Grand Rapids Press*, June 22, 1912.
2. Bust of Henry Wadsworth Longfellow.
3. Henry Wadsworth Longfellow, "The Builders," in *Henry Wadsworth Longfellow Complete Works* (East Sussex: Delphi Classics, 2012).

Chapter 1

4. Lucius Lyon survey notes. Copy held in Grand Rapids City Archives and Records Center.
5. *Historical Collections and Researches Made by the Michigan Pioneer and Historical Society*. Vol. 27 (1897).
6. Ibid.
7. Ibid.
8. Ibid.
9. Ibid.
10. John Almy, *State of Michigan—1845—To Emigrants* (1845).
11. Ibid.
12. Wright Lewis Coffinberry, *Autobiography of Wright L. Coffinberry* (1887), accessed May 24, 2022, University of Michigan Bentley Historical Library.

13. Wright Lewis Coffinberry, unpublished diary, March 17, 1855, accessed May 24, 2022, University of Michigan Bentley Historical Library.

Chapter 2

14. Albert Baxter, *History of Grand Rapids* (New York and Grand Rapids: Munsell, 1891).
15. Mark Twain, *The Gilded Age: A Tale of Today* (Chicago: American Publishing Company, 1873).
16. Laura Dassow Wells, *Henry David Thoreau: A Life* (Chicago: University of Chicago Press, 2017).
17. Baxter, *History of Grand Rapids*.
18. "Congressman Ford Answers the Charge," *Evening Leader* (Grand Rapids, MI), October 1, 1888.
19. "To See His Mother," *Evening Press* (Grand Rapids, MI), December 9, 1907.
20. "No More Chop Suey," *Grand Rapids Press*, May 12, 1908.
21. "Robinson's History Rewritten in 1916," *Grand Rapids Press*, August 13, 1918.
22. "Estimates 3,500 Alien Women Here," *Grand Rapids Press*, 1918.
23. "For Humanity to Be Slogan for Red Cross," *Grand Rapids Press*, 1917.

Chapter 3

24. "Landmark to Pass When City Closes East Side Powel Canal, Pioneer Hope for Great Future," *Grand Rapids Press*, November 27, 1925.
25. *Connections Along the Grand River* (pamphlet), Grand Valley State University, 2020.
26. "Landmark to Pass."
27. William T. Powers, letter to Grand Rapids Common Council, January 1904, accessed June 16, 2022, Grand Rapids City Archives and Records Center.
28. "Workaday River, Long Abused, May Beautify the City," *Grand Rapids Press*, June 18, 1927.
29. "Grand River: Better Days for Bedraggled Cinderella," *Grand Rapids Press*, 1970

Chapter 4

30. Carl Sandburg, *Ever the Winds of Change* (Chicago: University of Illinois Press, 1999.

31. Oak Hill building plans, 1890. Grand Rapids City Archives and Records Center.

32. "The Library and Its Needs," *Grand Rapids Press*, May 8, 1989.

33. "From Pillar to Post," *Grand Rapids Press*, August 16, 1894.

34. "Freedom Homes Starts First House," *Grand Rapids Press*, June 8, 1968.

Chapter 5

35. Baxter, *History of Grand Rapids*.

36. Ibid.

37. "Dog Pound Is a Disgrace to City," *Grand Rapids Herald*, 1904.

38. "Warrant Issued for Dog Catcher," *Grand Rapids Herald*, 1904.

39. "Why a Dog Pound At All?" *Grand Rapids Press*, 1904.

40. "Why Pick On the Dogs?" *Grand Rapids Herald*, 1916.

Chapter 6

41. "Retailers to Aid War Food Saving Organize," *Grand Rapids Press*, March 26, 1918.

42. Ibid.

43. Baxter, *History of Grand Rapids*.

44. Theodore O. Williams, *Survey Book 1* (1890), accessed June 16, 2022, Grand Rapids City Archives and Records Center.

45. *Report of the Dairy and Food Commissioner of the State of Michigan* (Lansing: Robert-Smith Printing, 1896), accessed September 21, 2022, via Archive.org.

46. Ibid.

47. "Food All Pure Here," *Grand Rapids Press*, September 27, 1900.

48. Grand Rapids City Commission proceedings, 1903, accessed June 16, 2022, Grand Rapids City Archives and Records Center.

49. Thomas Aquinas Major, letter to City Commission, August 7, 1928, accessed June 16, 2022, Grand Rapids City Archives and Records Center

50. *Annual Report of the Secretary of the State Horticultural Society of Michigan,* Michigan State Horticultural Society, Cornell University, 1875, accessed September 21, 2022 via Archive.org.
51. "Coffee Serving Art," *Grand Rapids Press*, December 24, 1899.

Chapter 7

52. "Banks Saved by Confession," *Kalamazoo Gazette*, October 30, 1903.

Chapter 8

53. "Winning Playground Sculpture for Festival Is Big Plastic Button," *Grand Rapids Press*, 1976.
54. "Art in Grand Rapids," *Grand Rapids Press*, 1909.
55. "The Status of Legend," *Flint Journal*, 1993.
56. *The Art in City Hall* (pamphlet), Municipal Art Advisory Commission, 1978, accessed June 16, 2022, Grand Rapids City Archives and Records Center.

Chapter 9

57. "Captain W.L. Coffinberry," *Evening Leader*, March 26, 1889.

ABOUT THE AUTHOR

Matthew A. Ellis is a lifelong resident of Grand Rapids, having lived in Eastown until he moved to the Boston Square neighborhood in 2020 with his wife, Ashley. Matthew has worked for the City of Grand Rapids Archives and Records Center since 2015 and graduated from Johns Hopkins University in 2020 with a MA in public management. He spearheaded a project for the city archives to digitize and publish records online and has presented on the city archives' collection of police mug shots. Matthew has served as a trustee for the Grand Rapids Historical Society since 2018 and has worked with the local history community in putting on programs and publishing articles. He is an avid reader and can often be found reading in his favorite local coffee shops around town. His most avid fans are his four huskies Xander, Indigo, Eros and Green Bean, but only when he has dog treats for them.

Visit us at
www.historypress.com